This is a textbook based on the research materials (HCO Bulletins) of Lafayette Ronald Hubbard, held copyright by the Church of Spiritual Technology, 419 North Larchmont, #162, Los Angeles, California, as well as the online Basic Study Manual by Rolf "Clearbird" Krause. Hubbard's research materials contain, but are not limited to, specific ideas, discoveries, principles, concepts, and methods of operation, which are separable from the wording used therein; they are in the public domain, and therefore not subject to copyright under Canadian and United States intellectual property law. This book is an overview of these ideas, discoveries, principles, concepts, and methods.

Title 17, Chapter 1, Section 102(b) of the Copyright Act (U.S.A.) states, "In no case does copyright protection for an original work of authorship extend to any idea, procedure, process, system, method of operation, concept, principle, or discovery, regardless of the form in which it is described, explained, illustrated, or embodied in such work." Similar precedents apply in Canadian common law.

Copyright (c) 2012 by N. Edward Matavka

Typeset by
Matavka Enterprises
1591, South Parade Court,
Unit 21,
Mississauga, Ontario,
Canada.

ISBN 978-0-9917682-0-2
F I R S T   E D I T I O N

# POINTS SYSTEM
## for The Student/Supervisor Hat Course

Written materials, per page - 0 rated.............3 pts
Written materials, per page - * rated.............5 "
Misunderstood from materials found, cleared.......1 "
Keywords on checksheet cleared....................3 "
Demo done, per checksheet.........................3 "
Demo done, not on checksheet......................1 "
Clay demo, per checksheet.........................25 "
Clay demo, not on checksheet......................5 "
Tape or video, per minute, 0-rated................1 "
Tape or video, per tape, * rated..................15 "
Essay per checksheet..............................10 "
Word clearing on other student, per word..........3 "
Twin check-out, regardless of result..............5 "
Written exam passed...............................200 "
Attest to theory or practical section.............100 "
Practical, not otherwise covered, per hr..........60 "
Coaching another student, same points as student

# PINK SHEET

DATE: \_\_\_\_/\_\_\_\_/_____

STUDENT: _____  COURSE: _____
SUPERVISOR: _____  SCHOOL: _____

```
SUPER | COACH | ASSIGN'T | OBSERVATIONS
------+-------+----------+------------------
      |       |          |
      |       |_____|_____
      |       |_____|_____
      |       |_____|_____
      |       |_____|_____
      |       |_____|_____
      |       |_____|_____
      |       |_____|_____
      |       |_____|_____
      |       |_____|_____
      |       |_____|_____
      |       |_____|_____
      |       |_____|_____
      |       |_____|_____
      |       |_____|_____
      |       |_____|_____
      |       |_____|_____
      |       |_____|_____
      |       |_____|_____
      |       |_____|_____
      |       |_____|_____
      |       |_____|_____
      |       |_____|_____
      |       |_____|_____
      |       |_____|_____
      |       |_____|_____
      |       |_____|_____
```

Checksheet
for The Student Hat Course

HAT: On a train, a locomotive driver and a conductor each wear a different kind of hat. You will notice that various jobs in this society are designated by different hats. From this, we get the word 'hat' as an informal term meaning one's specialised duties.

Name: _____
School: _____
Date started: ____ / ____ / _____
Date completed: ____ / ____ / _____

PREREQUISITES: None.

MATERIALS: - The Student Hat Course Pack

LENGTH OF COURSE: Six months (sixty minutes per day); three months (120 minutes per day)

IDEAL SCENE: Ideally, the end product of this course is an able student who knows how to study, has the knowledge and tools to be able to study and apply the materials of any course, and uses this knowledge.

SEQUENCE: This checksheet is studied once through, in the sequence listed thereon.

REALITY FACTOR: YOU ARE EXPECTED TO APPLY THE STUDY TECHNOLOGY AS YOU LEARN IT TO YOUR IMMEDIATE STUDIES. YOU ARE EXPECTED TO DEMONSTRATE YOUR ABILITY TO APPLY THE COURSE MATERIALS BY USING THE STUDY TECH ON THE COURSE ITSELF.

You must see for yourself whether this data is true or not through direct application. A datum is true because it works and because you have seen that it is true, not just because someone says it is true.

The value of your future studies is dependent upon how well you do on this course. A good, practical grasp of these materials will ensure your success in all future study.

Whenever a theory item on a checksheet is marked with a star (*), it means the item is to be star-rate checked out. A star-rate check-out is defined as "a very exact checkout which verifies the full and minute knowledge of the student of a portion of study materials and tests his full understanding of the data and ability to apply it." A checkout is done either by another student or, on selected issues, by the Supervisor (teacher) himself.

NOTE: a) When answering an essay question, the student should explain the idea in HIS OWN WORDS. Doing otherwise, in addition to being plagiarism (an academic offence), shows that the student does not conceptually understand the answer, and is grounds for a fail.

## SECTION I.  ORIENTATION(#)

(#) The below items are to be checked out by the Supervisor only.

\*    1. Read GLOSSARY.                             \_\_\_\_

\*    2. Read WHY STUDY.                            \_\_\_\_

\*    3. Read THE POINTS SYSTEM.                    \_\_\_\_

    4. ESSAY. What is the primary              \_\_\_\_
       obstacle to learning?

    5. PRACTICAL. Think about someone          \_\_\_\_
       you have known who felt he already
       knew all about some subject. How
       would this attitude affect the
       person's ability to actually learn
       something new about that subject?

\*    6. Read PINK SHEETS.                          \_\_\_\_

\*    7. Read CHECKSHEETS.                          \_\_\_\_

\*    8. Read STAR-RATE CHECK-OUTS.                 \_\_\_\_

9. PRACTICAL. Check the supervisor ____
   out on material of your choice (2
   page minimum). The supervisor
   may make mistakes; if a mistake
   is made, the student must fail
   the Supervisor immediately or
   the student himself fails.

\* 10. Read TWINNING. ____

11. PRACTICAL.

    a) Twin up with another student ____
    for this practical.

    b) Have your twin give you a ____
    star-rate check-out on TWINNING.

    c) Give your twin a star-rate ____
    check-out on TWINNING.

12. ESSAY. Write up your ____
    responsibilities as a twin. Turn
    this in to your supervisor.

13. Scan REPRESENTATION OF CONCEPTS. ____
    Be sure you can do all kinds of
    demonstrations properly. (STUDENT
    ATTEST ONLY)

14. Read BUILDING UNDERSTANDING. ____

15. GRAPHIC DEMO.  Demonstrate          ____
    affinity.

16. GRAPHIC DEMO.  Demonstrate          ____
    reality.

17. GRAPHIC DEMO.  Demonstrate          ____
    communication.

18. ESSAY.  Explain ARC and how they    ____
    add up to understanding.  Turn it
    in to the supervisor.

19. GRAPHIC DEMO.  How understanding    ____
    relates to study.

20. PRACTICAL.  Notice some things      ____
    you have affinity for, reality
    about, or good communication
    with.  How well do you understand
    them?

21. Read GLIBNESS IN THE STUDENT.       ____

22. ESSAY.  How do you recognise a      ____
    glib student?

## SECTION II.  STUDY TECH

---
Congratulations! You may now be checked out by your twin or another student. Supervisor check-outs are done from here on in only if the checksheet says so, or if the supervisor wishes to gauge your progress.

---

    1. Read CONFUSIONS. \_\_\_\_

    2. PRACTICAL. Outside course, notice something you are confused about. Find or choose a stable datum about it, and then another. Notice what happens. \_\_\_\_

\*     3. Read RELAXATION AND STUDY. \_\_\_\_

    4. PRACTICAL. Sit down in a quiet place with closed eyes, and breathe deeply for four to five minutes. Then, study a few pages of text of your choice. What happened? \_\_\_\_

\*     5. Read THE PYRAMID OF KNOWLEDGE. \_\_\_\_

6. ESSAY. For a subject of your choice, write down its most basic data you know of, and three specific manifestations thereof. ____

\*   7. Read REPRESENTATION OF CONCEPTS. ____

8. ESSAY. Give examples of the mass in five different subjects. Turn your write-up in to the Supervisor. ____

9. ESSAY. How do you recognise lack of mass? ____

10. ESSAY. Choose some activity or subject with which you are familiar. Give an example of a circumstance you might encounter in it, in which use of a demo kit might help you. Now, do the same thing, showing how sketches might help you work something out. Turn your write-up in to the Supervisor. ____

11. DEMO. Using a demo kit, show the basic purpose of same is, and how it helps a person to study something. ____

12. DEMO. How to cross the street safely. ____

13. GRAPHIC DEMO. The route you  \_\_\_\_
    take to get from course to home.

14. CLAY DEMO. Demonstrate a  \_\_\_\_
    hammer.

15. CLAY DEMO. Demonstrate a man.  \_\_\_\_

16. CLAY DEMO. Demonstrate a man  \_\_\_\_
    thinking of a tree.

\* 17. Read THE GRADIENT OF STUDY.  \_\_\_\_

18. GRAPHIC DEMO. How to handle a  \_\_\_\_
    steep gradient

\* 19. Read THE MISUNDERSTOOD WORD.  \_\_\_\_

20. Read ENGLISH DIALECTS.  \_\_\_\_

21. CLAY DEMO. Demonstrate the  \_\_\_\_
    three barriers to study.

    a) Lack of mass.  \_\_\_\_

    b) Too steep a gradient.  \_\_\_\_

    c) A misunderstood word.  \_\_\_\_

\* 22. Read TYPES OF MISUNDERSTOODS.  \_\_\_\_

23. PRACTICAL. Give an example of each of the following to the Supervisor. _____

    a) A false definition. _____

    b) An invented definition. _____

    c) An incorrect definition. _____

    d) An incomplete definition. _____

    e) An unsuitable definition. _____

    f) A substitute (homonymic) definition. _____

    g) An omitted (missing) definition. _____

    h) A non-definition. _____

24. ESSAY. Write up five different examples of how a word could be misunderstood or not understood. Turn your essay in to the Supervisor. _____

25. Read SUGGESTED DICTIONARIES. _____

26. PRACTICAL. Look up a word in ____
    some of the suggested dictionaries.
    Then, look it up in a dinky
    dictionary. Compare the dinky
    dictionary to the big dictionaries.

27. PRACTICAL. Pick an encyclo- ____
    paedia or other reference book
    from the course room. Look
    through it until you find a word
    you do not understand. Look it up
    in at least four dictionaries,
    preferably the ones recommended
    here. If you find yourself running
    into too many words in the
    definitions you do not understand,
    clear them up in a simpler
    dictionary. Based on this
    exercise, determine which
    dictionary is the correct gradient
    for you and suits your needs best.
    When done, write up what you did
    and turn your write-up in to the
    Supervisor.

28. PRACTICAL. Do the following ____
    to familiarise yourself with using
    a dictionary:

    a) Take a dictionary you have ____
    selected in the previous practical
    exercise.

b) Use the guide words at the _____
top of each page to help you find
the word "sail".

c) Look up the pronunciation of _____
the word.

d) Notice what part of speech is _____
given for the first definition.

e) Read the first definition and _____
any examples given for it.

f) Read over the rest of the _____
definitions. Note if any are
specialised or slang.

g) Read the derivation. _____

h) Read any idioms, synonyms, _____
or notes on usage given.

i) Repeat the above steps for _____
the words dream, fight, wood,
and graduate.

29. Read CLEARING WORDS. _____

30. ESSAY. How do you clear a word? _____

31. PRACTICAL. Find another student. \_\_\_\_
    Do Basic Word Clearing on that
    person.

32. ESSAY.  What is Reading Aloud     \_\_\_\_
    Word Clearing?

33. Find someone who could benefit    \_\_\_\_
    from Reading Aloud Word Clearing.
    Do it to a satisfactory end
    result.

34. PRACTICAL.                        \_\_\_\_

    a) Read ahead in your course      \_\_\_\_
    pack and find a word you know
    you don't know the meaning of.

    b) Use Simple Word Clearing to    \_\_\_\_
    get its meaning as used.

    c) Compare your understanding of  \_\_\_\_
    the word now to when you first
    found the word in your course
    pack.

    d) Repeat the above, but this     \_\_\_\_
    time, find a word in your course
    pack which you are not <u>totally</u>
    certain that you understand.

e) Use Simple Word Clearing to      ____
get its meaning as used.

f) Compare your understanding of    ____
the word now to when you first
found the word in your course
pack.

g) Now, find a word in your         ____
course pack you understand in the
context it is being used,
but for which there are other
definitions you don't know.

h) Use Simple Word Clearing to      ____
get its meaning as used.

i) Compare your understanding of    ____
the word now to when you first found
the word in your course pack.

j) Write up what you have learned   ____
from this practical exercise and
turn your write-up in to the
Supervisor.

35. Read FORMS OF STUDY.            ____

36. ESSAY. When might a live lecture ____
    be best? When might a recording
    be best?

\*   37. Read NOMENCLATURE. \_\_\_\_

    38. ESSAY. Why are nomenclatures \_\_\_\_
        needed in specialised fields?

    39. CLAY DEMO. A nomenclature not \_\_\_\_
        understood is a barrier to com-
        munication.

    40. PRACTICAL. Make a list of the \_\_\_\_
        nomenclature used in each of the
        areas you are studying. Define
        each. Keep this list.

\*   41. Read DOUBLE-SPEAK. \_\_\_\_

    42. ESSAY. Why is double-speak so \_\_\_\_
        common in politics?

    43. PRACTICAL. Read a recent news- \_\_\_\_
        paper. Find an example of each
        type of double-speak.

\*   44. Read BALANCE IN STUDY. \_\_\_\_

\*   45. Read LEVELS OF ENGAGEMENT. \_\_\_\_

    46. DEMO. Each of the eight levels \_\_\_\_
        of engagement with a subject,

47. ESSAY. In your estimation, which____
    subjects are you engaged in the
    study of, and on what level are
    you engaged with each?

48. Read OUT-POINTS AND PLUS-POINTS. ____

49. PRACTICAL. Read a recent news-  ____
    paper. Find five out-points and
    five plus-points.

    FINAL DRILL AND PRACTICAL

50. PRACTICAL

    a) Review your Student Hat      ____
    Course pack and make a list on a
    sheet of paper of every  study
    tool and remedy mentioned, such
    as the first obstacle to overcome
    in study, gradients, clay
    demonstrations, sketching, &c.
    You should have at least twenty-
    five items on this list by the time
    you have reviewed your pack.

    b) Using the list of study tech  ____
    tools you have compiled above,
    write down the tools or remedies
    you would apply in each of the
    following situations and the
    specific actions you would take

in applying them.

i) You are reading a book     ____
at home and find yourself
doping off.

ii) You are studying on       ____
course and the material you
are reading gets confusing.

iii) You are sitting at your  ____
desk trying to work out a
new design for something.

iiii) You are trying to clear a ____
word in a dictionary, but
after reading the
definition that fits the
context of the word, you
still don't understand
it fully.

iv) You are trying to learn   ____
how to use a large,
complex piece of
machinery.

v) You are listening to a     ____
recorded lesson, and you
hear something you find
unbelievable.

vi) You are attempting to    ____
repair your motorcycle;
while reading the repair
manual, you come across
some terms that are not
defined in the manual
or in a dictionary.

vii) Your friend is taking a
course in type-writing,
but says she already
knows how to do this.

viii) You are attempting to    ____
learn how to use your
new computer, but there
is something in the
owner's manual which
makes no sense to you.

ix) You are getting into a    ____
lot of word chains with
the dictionary you are
using.

x) You are learning how to
do something new at work,
but are very confused.

When done, turn your write-ups in to the Supervisor.

Checksheet
for The Supervisor Hat Course

HAT: On a train, a locomotive driver and a conductor each wear a different kind of hat. You will notice that various jobs in this society are designated by different hats. From this, we get the word 'hat' as an informal term meaning one's specialised duties.

Name: _____
School: _____
Date started: ____ / ____ / _____
Date completed: ____ / ____ / _____

PREREQUISITES: - The Student Hat Course
    (HIGHLY RECOMMENDED!)
- Education as expert in field

MATERIALS: - The Student Hat Course Pack
- The Supervisor Hat Course Pack

LENGTH OF COURSE: Six weeks full-time (four hours per day, five days per week)

IDEAL SCENE: Ideally, the end product of this course is an effective course supervisor, who knows how to apply Study Technology on his students, ensures course discipline, and can properly manage a course according to the rules of Study Technology. This course is not a replacement for a supervisor who is an expert in his field; however, it can be used by itself to train _locum tenens_ supervisors.

SEQUENCE: This checksheet is studied once through, in the sequence listed thereon.

You must see for yourself whether this data is true or not through direct application. A datum is true because it works and because you have seen that it is true, not just because someone says it is true.

Whenever a theory item on a checksheet is marked with a star (*), it means the item is to be star-rate checked out. A star-rate check-out is defined as "a very exact checkout which verifies the full and minute knowledge of the student of a portion of study materials and tests his full understanding of the data and ability to apply it." A checkout is done either by another student or, on selected issues, by the Supervisor (teacher) himself.

NOTE: When answering an essay question, the student should explain the idea in HIS OWN WORDS. Doing otherwise, in addition to being plagiarism (an academic offence), shows that the student does not conceptually understand the answer, and is grounds for a fail.

## SECTION I.  ORIENTATION(#)

\*       1. Read GLOSSARY.                            \_\_\_\_\_

\*       2. Read TWINNING.                            \_\_\_\_\_

\*       3. Read THE POINTS SYSTEM.                   \_\_\_\_\_

\*       4. Read CHECKSHEETS.                         \_\_\_\_\_

\*      5. Read STAR-RATE CHECK-OUTS.                    ____

       5. Check your Supervisor out on material of ____
          your choice (at least 2 pages long). He
          may, or may not, make a mistake (such as
          an incorrect answer, poor demonstration,
          or hesitation in speech). The student
          must fail his Supervisor immediately after
          the mistake, otherwise he himself fails.

       6. Scan REPRESENTATION OF CONCEPTS. Be sure____
          you can do all kinds of demonstrations
          properly. (STUDENT ATTEST ONLY)

       7. Read BUILDING UNDERSTANDING.                   ____

       8. GRAPHIC DEMO. Demonstrate affinity.            ____

       9. GRAPHIC DEMO. Demonstrate reality.             ____

       10. GRAPHIC DEMO. Demonstrate communication.____

       11. ESSAY. Explain ARC and how it adds up    ____
           to understanding. Turn it in to the
           supervisor.

       12. GRAPHIC DEMO. How understanding relates ____
           to study.

\*      13. Read GLIBNESS IN THE STUDENT.                ____

       14. ESSAY. How to catch and destroy glibness____
           in a student.

15. CLAY DEMO. Use clay to model why          ____
    glibness is incompatible with good study
    skills. Instructions to be provided by
    the Supervisor.

*   16. Read CONFUSIONS.                       ____

    17. ESSAY. What are stable data and why    ____
        should the student find the right ones?

    18. PRACTICAL. Outside course, notice      ____
        something you are confused about. Find
        or choose a stable datum about it, and
        then another. Notice what happens.

*   19. Read RELAXATION AND STUDY.             ____

    20. PRACTICAL. Sit or lie down in a quiet  ____
        place with eyes shut, and breathe deeply
        for four or five minutes. Then, study
        a few pages of text of your choice.

    21. GRAPHIC DEMO. Why it is important to   ____
        study in a quiet space.

*   22. Read THE PYRAMID OF KNOWLEDGE.         ____

    23. ESSAY. For a subject of your choice,   ____
        write down its most basic data you know
        of, and three specific manifestations
        thereof.

*   24. Read REPRESENTATION OF CONCEPTS.       ____

25. ESSAY.  Choose some activity or subject     ____
    with which you are familiar.  Give an
    example of a circumstance you might
    encounter in it, in which use of a demo
    kit might help you.  Now, do the same
    thing, showing how sketches might help
    you work something out.  Turn your
    write-up in to the Supervisor.

26. DEMO.  Using a demo kit, show what the     ____
    basic purpose of same is, and how it helps
    a person to study something.

27. DEMO.  How to cross the street safely.     ____
    Present your demonstration to the class.

28. CLAY DEMO.  Demonstrate a hammer.          ____
    Present your demonstration to the class.

29. CLAY DEMO.  Demonstrate a man.             ____
    Present your demonstration to the class.

30. CLAY DEMO.  Demonstrate a man thinking     ____
    of a tree.  Present your demonstration
    to the class.

31. ESSAY.  The different ways we provide      ____
    mass on a course to go with the
    significance.

\*   32. Read THE GRADIENT OF STUDY.              ____

33. GRAPHIC DEMO. How to handle a steep        ____
    gradient.

34. ESSAY.  How to detect and handle a       _____
    student with a skipped gradient.

\*   35. Read THE MISUNDERSTOOD WORD.              _____

36. ESSAY.  How to detect and handle someone _____
    with a misunderstood morpheme.

\*   37. Read ENGLISH DIALECTS.                    _____

38. CLAY DEMO.  Demonstrate the three        _____
    barriers to study.

    a) Lack of mass.                         _____

    b) Too steep a gradient.                 _____

    c) A misunderstood word.                 _____

\*   39. Read TYPES OF MISUNDERSTOODS.             _____

40. PRACTICAL. Give an example of each of the_____
    following to the Supervisor.

    a) A false definition.                   _____

    b) An invented definition.               _____

    c) An incorrect definition.              _____

    d) An incomplete definition.             _____

    e) An unsuitable definition.             _____

    f) A substitute (homonymic) definition. \_\_\_\_

    g) An omitted (missing) definition. \_\_\_\_

    h) A non-definition. \_\_\_\_

41. ESSAY. Write up five different examples \_\_\_\_ of how a word could be misunderstood or not understood. Turn your essay in to the Supervisor.

42. Read SUGGESTED DICTIONARIES. \_\_\_\_

43. PRACTICAL. Look up a word in some of \_\_\_\_ the suggested dictionaries. Then, look it up in a dinky dictionary. Compare the dinky dictionary to the big dictionaries.

44. Read CLEARING WORDS. \_\_\_\_

45. ESSAY. How do you clear a word? \_\_\_\_

46. ESSAY. What is Reading Aloud Word \_\_\_\_ Clearing?

47. Find someone who could benefit from \_\_\_\_ Reading Aloud Word Clearing. Do it to a satisfactory end result.

48. Read FORMS OF STUDY. \_\_\_\_

49. PRACTICAL. When might a live lecture be \_\_\_\_ best? When might a recording be best?

|   |   |   |
|---|---|---|
|   | 49. Read NOMENCLATURE. | ____ |
|   | 50. ESSAY. Why are nomenclatures needed in specialised fields? | ____ |
|   | 51. PRACTICAL. Make a list of the nomenclature of your field of expertise. Define each term. Keep this list. | ____ |
|   | 52. CLAY DEMO. A nomenclature not understood is a barrier to communication. | ____ |
| * | 53. Read DOUBLE-SPEAK. | ____ |
|   | 54. ESSAY. Why is double-speak so common in politics? | ____ |
|   | 55. PRACTICAL. Read a recent newspaper. Find an example of each type of double=speak. | ____ |
| * | 56. Read BALANCE IN STUDY. | ____ |
| * | 57. Read LEVELS OF ENGAGEMENT. | ____ |
|   | 58. DEMO. Each of the eight levels of engagement with a subject. | ____ |
|   | 59. ESSAY. In your estimation, which subjects are you engaged in the study of, and what level are you studying on with each? | ____ |
|   | 60. Read OUT-POINTS AND PLUS-POINTS. | ____ |

61. PRACTICAL. Read a recent newspaper. \_\_\_\_
    Find ten out-points and ten plus-points.

\* 62. Read PINK SHEETS: A SUPERVISOR'S \_\_\_\_
    PERSPECTIVE.

63. PRACTICAL: Find a pair of twins. Have \_\_\_\_
    them coach each other on material of your
    choice. Observe and write your
    observations on a pink sheet. Assign
    work if necessary. Follow up.

\* 64. Read WHAT IS A COURSE? \_\_\_\_

\* 65. Read RUNNING A COURSE. \_\_\_\_

66. GRAPHIC DEMO. Sketch a course run with \_\_\_\_
    ethics in, and a course run with ethics out.

67. Read LEVELS OF ENGAGEMENT. \_\_\_\_

68. ESSAY. How does the professional \_\_\_\_
    differ from the simple practitioner?

\* 69. Read OUT-POINTS AND PLUS-POINTS. \_\_\_\_

70. ESSAY. If a course pack has many \_\_\_\_
    out-points, what does this translate
    into, from a practical, Supervisory
    standpoint?

71. Read WRITING COURSE MATERIALS. \_\_\_\_

72. ESSAY. Do you see yourself ever writing ____ a set of course materials? If yes, at which stage would you consider yourself competent to do so?

# Contents

1  Why Study                                11

2  Pink Sheets                              17

3  Checksheets                              23
   3.1  Star-Rate Check-Outs . . . . . . . .  26

4  The Eight Dynamics                       35

5  Twinning                                 43

6  Building Understanding                   49

7  Glibness in the Student                  59

# CONTENTS

| | | |
|---|---|---|
| 8 | Confusions | 63 |
| 9 | Relaxation and Study | 69 |
| 10 | The Pyramid of Knowledge | 73 |
| 11 | Representation of Concepts | 77 |
| 12 | The Gradient of Study | 87 |
| 13 | The Misunderstood Word | 91 |
| | 13.1 Types of Misunderstoods | 103 |
| | 13.2 Suggested Dictionaries | 108 |
| | 13.3 Clearing Words | 114 |
| 14 | Forms of Study | 117 |
| 15 | Nomenclature | 121 |
| | 15.1 Double-Speak | 125 |
| 16 | Balance in Study | 129 |
| 17 | Levels of Engagement | 135 |
| 18 | Out-points and Plus-points | 141 |

| CONTENTS | 3 |
|---|---|
| 19 What is a Course? | 147 |
| 20 Running a Course | 155 |
| 21 The Points System | 159 |
| 22 Pink Sheets: A Supervisor's Perspective | 163 |
| 23 Writing Course Materials | 169 |

CONTENTS

# Introduction

On a train, a locomotive engineer and a conductor each wears a different kind of hat. One will notice that various jobs in the society are designated by different hats. From this, we get the word "hat" as a slang term meaning one's specialised duties. One can wear various hats, switching between them in the course of his life, and being differently proficient at 'wearing' each; a lawyer may, for instance, wear the hats of lawyer, father, husband, student, and teacher.

This course, entitled the Student Hat Course, was originally compiled by Lafayette Ronald Hubbard (hereinafter known as L.R.H.), science fiction author and founder of the system of beliefs and practices known as Scientology. It was originally intended solely for internal use; however, it is easily applicable in other fields as well, as long as it is edited to conform better to general learning. While this book was being written, the author used the principles of Hubbard's original course to assist him in writing. Similarly, the Hat Course is *self-applicable*; the student can use the Hat Course to learn the Hat Course.

L.R.H. was a prolific and a genius; in addition to his work on education and his ecclesiastical role, he discovered a new method for psychotherapy, a system of ethics, a new way of managing a business (by statistics), and many other concepts. It was evidently Hubbard's intent to make his non-fiction work a gift to Mankind, free for all to use and change. Unfortunately, the management structure of the organisations he created to protect his work later became corrupt and greedy.

Currently, Hubbard's work is sold at a high price by a monolithic entity, the Church of Scientology, and a complex network of subsidiaries and front groups. One of these subsidiaries, the Religious Technology Center, has even managed to trademark Hubbard's preferred form of his name. These groups sell only an altered version of Hubbard's work (concentrating on the psychotherapeutic aspect), but repeatedly and fraudulently claim that they are the sole group selling the 'real deal'. Furthermore, for financial reasons (specifically, income tax exemption in the United States of America), these groups repeatedly and falsely claim that they constitute a religion; the reality is that they are nothing more or less than a for-profit business selling over-priced psychotherapy.

This book is a textbook on the system of education developed by Hubbard. His research papers, the so-called *HCO Bulletins*, were collected and the educational data was picked out of them, expanded and paraphrased. The aforementioned organisations greatly fear alternative textbooks on Hubbard's discoveries; they point to Hubbard's own writings, which spoke out against critical 'treatments' of a work. The hypocrisy of their stance is quite stunning, since Bridge Publications, a front group for the Church of Scientology, has in fact published multiple such treatments of Hubbard's study method; furthermore, the Church of Scientology itself has done the same with *The Scientology Handbook*, a sort of user's manual to life. The simple truth is that if these corporations permit textbooks to be published, their monopoly on this great man's works will come to an end; therefore, they fight tooth and nail to appease their only god, the Almighty Dollar.

Another reason this book was written is simply that the research papers, though written in a very clear, easy-to-understand style, were published in no particular order. Further, some of them include things that were later retracted in a later bulletin. This may be fine for an advanced student with all the necessary materials, or a student taking an organised class on how to study, in which the instructor can xerox whichever bulletins are needed, but it is definitely not fine for a beginning student who has no access to Hubbard's research papers.

Hubbard's research papers were only one source from which this manual was compiled; they were selected in accordance with a checksheet authored by Dan Koon. There were two other sources that were drawn from directly to fill in the blanks in Hubbard's papers. Their story needs telling, as it shows the attitude that pervades anything involving the late, great Hubbard.

Having been impressed by Hubbard's techniques and disillusioned by the corporations 'protecting' them, a Dane named Rolf Krause took it upon himself to write several textbooks on his discoveries, including Hubbardian psychotherapy (also known as auditing). Fearing retribution by lawyers, Krause pseudonymously (as Clearbird) published his manuals on multiple sites throughout the World Wide Web, making them available for free. This manual is based partly on Krause's rendition of Hubbard's work, known as the *Clearbird Study Manual*.

The third variant of the Student Hat is known as the *Study Basics Course*; it was written anonymously in 1992. The author no doubt has good reason to seek anonymity; the retribution he may face were his identity to be revealed could be financially ruinous. His identity remains unknown to this day, twenty years later. The material adapted from this source includes the chapters on *glibness, confusions, relaxation and study,* the *pyramid of knowledge*, and *double-speak*.

The aim of this book is to have compiled a workable, coherent system for the study of any subject. There is, however, an assumption underlying this system, and that is that whatever the Student Hat Course is being applied to makes sense, is written coherently, and that it is itself workable. If this assumption is broken and the Student Hat is applied regardless, nothing can or will result other than insanity and lack of proper perspective. The Student Hat was not designed, despite the words of some loud, but ignorant, critics, to be a means of mind control or brainwashing. Hubbard simply failed to emphasise (although he mentioned it) that the Student Hat was only to be used on materials that presented a workable subject and were written to a high standard.

The author is not an adherent of Scientology; although he does indeed practice many of the methods and concepts discovered by L.R.H., he does not belong to any organisation, formal or informal, of like-minded people. Furthermore, nothing in Hubbard's papers or tapes has influenced the author's religious views in any way whatever. The story is simply that having been recommended Hubbard's study materials by an acquaintance, the author found that they worked. It is the author's hope that the student will similarly find that they work. The student must see for himself whether or not this course is true or not through direct application. A datum is true because *it works* and the student has *seen* that it is true, and not because someone tells him so.

This book attempts to preserve the original style of learning, as written on Hubbard's loose-leaf research papers; therefore, it similarly uses a check-sheet. Under a check-sheet system, the student is to do the tasks listed on the sheet, and as each one is done, he can present himself to a second student, or to the teacher or course supervisor, who is to examine his knowledge of said task.

The author, in addition, does not profess to having devised or originated this system of learning. It is the invention of LaFayette Ronald Hubbard, who, in turn, adapted it from *Elements of Composition and Rhetoric* by Virginia Waddy, a teacher of rhetoric at Richmond High School Virginia, as well as from the teaching methods of Charles and

Ava Berner. Hubbard's method was then, in turn, copied by Rolf Krause and the anonymous author mentioned above, as well as the anonymous editors working at Bridge Publications.

Furthermore, this book is not an attempt to impress feminists. What is meant by this is that, throughout the book, the student, as well as the teacher, is referred to by the masculine singular pronoun ("he"). It has not escaped the author's attention that female students exist; however, it would look very inelegant to address the student as "s/he", or, even worse, as "them". No offense is intended toward the student, and none should be taken.

# Chapter 1
# Why Study

Although modern society places a great amount of emphasis on education, with a wide array of books being written on almost every subject that can be studied, there has been one very notable exception: that of education itself. Although books have been written about how teachers are to teach, and what will be on the examination, only a very few texts exist on the process of studying *per se*, and fewer still that recommend a method for doing so. This book attempts to remedy this problem, at least partially.

Certainly, there have been some methods devised that claim to increase the percentage of retention; however, what the authors of such methods, such as what is known as speed-reading, fail to understand is that there is no acceptable percentage of retention. Studying is not to be regarded as simply reading—an activity where one goes through a certain number of words, some of them stick, and one achieves a desirable benefit from this.

Understanding and application are not understanding and application unless they are done to their logical conclusion (that is, 100%). Either one understands and does it, or does not understand and does not do it. To press the blue button does not mean to pull the red handle; to service the brakes does not mean to rotate the tyres. If one does not understand the subject, he will not last long in any practical field. Some subjects are more forgiving, and will allow impostors in without anyone noticing; this does not change the fact that understanding is either there or not there. Application works the same way; one will not have success as an automobile mechanic if he only repairs

50% of automobiles.

Before one learns *how* to study, it is very important to correctly recognise *why* they are studying, and to break down the numerous barriers that prevent useful material from being retained in memory. If this is not done, it is probable that the student will look at his opportunity from the wrong perspective: namely, that he needs the information to pass a particular examination, and not that he needs it to accomplish something. Consequently, the student will likely be able to regurgitate prepared answers to questions asked, but with no understanding or ability to apply his knowledge to solve problems.

The first barrier to be overcome is *unwillingness to learn*. If the student has no interest in, or willingness to learn, the knowledge at hand, he will end up "studying for the examination." In other words, the student will be asking himself 'How will I repeat this when asked a question about it?', or 'How will I pass the exam?'.

An example, drawn from the world of law, will illustrate. Swamped by work, an experienced barrister hires an assistant, straight from university.

Nothing comes from the partnership except arguments and a lack of success. The reason for this is that the young student knows nothing about his field, and that the elder lawyer does not know why. The young student has been studying his materials so that he could be examined on them, not so that he can argue in court. The more experienced man may not be superior in the long run, but he most certainly knows how to plead his case: even though he uses the same material as his junior, his study is on the basis of how he *applies* this to his career. Every time the senior lawyer picks up his books, he asks the same question as he reads: 'How does this apply to my case?'

This is the fundamental difference between academic and applied study, and this is why some people, after graduation with honours, fail in the field. As illustrated previously, instead of looking at data and inquiring about whether it will be on the quiz, it would be far better to ask how it applies to one's chosen career path, or what one is doing in general. By thinking along these lines, the student will be better prepared to take advantage of his field of study.

Another barrier to study is arrogance in respect to one's abilities. One can not approach a subject labouring under the mistaken belief that *one knows everything about it to begin with.* A student who believes he knows everything about a subject will *not be able to learn* anything about it.

A student might already be acquainted with a subject, having previously studied it in some way; if, having had success in his field, he now has the idea that he knows all about it, he will essentially be studying through smoked glass. With this obstacle in the way, one can get stuck in his studies and not make forward progress; this is true for students of all subjects. If one can open his mind as regards his subject, he can overcome this hurdle and be able to learn. The student must also *intend* to learn; if he is not willing to learn, he will not get far with the subject.

# Chapter 2
# Pink Sheets

The gap between learning data and demonstrating the practical skills in the subject takes several huge steps. In training, the pink sheet system helps the student cross that gap. Receiving pink sheets as a student, seeing what one did wrong, and restudying that area, sharpens one's ability to apply Study Technology to oneself and to his twin, and allows him to wear his hat better.

The student is responsible for all the materials and courses he or she has studied earlier. If the student is unable to apply or use any of these materials, the supervisor can issue a pink sheet and have the student catch up on anything missed. A pink sheet should never develop into a long action, or into punishment. It is nothing, if not a quick and precise remedy to correct the student and get him back on track.

The course supervisor has a clipboard with pink sheet forms on it. A pink sheet master is included at the beginning of this package, before the checksheet; it is sufficient to send a student down to mimeo, ditto, or xerox the pink sheet master onto pink paper. The supervisor issues one of these when he sees that the student apparently has missed something. This can be as a result of a drill that causes trouble, any weak materials revealed by a check-out, or an examination. The supervisor can also do direct observations of students' study habits, or even their general behaviour, and issue a pink sheet based on his observations.

There are rules to writing a pink sheet, which should be known by students as well as by the supervisor. First of all, the supervisor must always make a carbon copy of any pink sheet he issues. He simply puts a sheet of carbon paper between two forms, writes on the top sheet, and gets a copy underneath, which he keeps for his own use. Second, the supervisor must always date and sign the pink sheet. The supervisor observes the student or a teaching session, standing close enough to see and hear. Third, he writes his observations in the appropriate column. He does not necessarily look for study and teaching errors at first; he simply records what is happening. He does not attempt to correct or to teach. He simply observes and records; it may result in no assignment at this point. The supervisor simply makes his presence known and shows interest in what is going on. He may write one or more pages of observations. Now, it is time to evaluate. The supervisor looks over what he has noted, and sees if anything needs correction; if he has found something, he fills in the assignment column, noting the exact materials to be studied. If no assignment has been given, the pink sheet is given to the student anyway; it may help. Finally, the original is given to the student, and the copy is filed in the supervisor's course folder. When completed, the original is filed in the student's folder.

## CHAPTER 2. PINK SHEETS

When a student has received a pink sheet assignment, it should be done with a twin, whether it is theory, practical, or both. The twin first reviews the observations with the student; then, he star-rates the student on the issues as assigned and drills the student until the correct data are completely learned and understood. Once this is done, the twin initials the column labelled COACH; the student is now ready to hand the pink sheet in to the supervisor.

The student now turns his pink sheet in to the supervisor. This must be done in person, as the supervisor may wish to go over it with the student and check him out himself. In doing this, the supervisor wishes to know if the pink sheet has done its job, or if he has to keep a closer eye on the student or do remedial work with him.

Pink sheets must never be used as punishment or to convince the student that he is wrong. They are used to improve the student's study or teaching ability by having him re-study data and do practical drills in the weak areas. A student's weakness in data and skills will often not show up under the normal conditions of theory study and practical drilling, but they will stand out very sharply when the time comes to apply what he has learned. Therefore, a pink sheet assignment does not necessarily mean that the student did not study the material properly, even if he has already passed it in theory or practical. It does mean that he has not learned it well enough to use it under the duress of an actual situation. If a student has gone a few days without receiving a pink sheet, he should start asking for one. Pink sheets ensure that study results in a string of certainties—the basic tenet of Study Technology. It may take several times over the material to be able to do things correctly, and under trying conditions, in practice.

# Chapter 3

# Checksheets

A *checksheet* is a printed form that sets out the items to be studied, or actions to be done, by a student, item by item, on a course. It lists all the materials of the course in the order they are to be studied. For each item, there is a line for the student, or his twin, to initial and date; this is called an *attest*. The student must not attest on an item until he knows, and can apply, the data.

Some items must be checked out in a very exact, deep fashion, and they must be checked out by another (usually by the twin, but sometimes instead by the supervisor) to ensure reliability. These are called star-rate check-outs; they are marked with a star on the checksheet itself. Furthermore, there are items that must be checked out *only* by the Supervisor; these can be zero-rate or star-rate, but they will always be marked, SUPERVISOR CHECK-OUT.

When the supervisor, or another student, attests on a star-rated item, it means that he has given the student a star-rate check-out on the item, and that the student has passed. The supervisor *must* inspect students' checksheets every day, so as to ensure that all students are following the checksheet in the right order and that they are making good progress.

The materials are laid-out on the checksheet in the best and most logical order for study, so the student covers all the materials on a good gradient. Following the exact order of the checksheet also helps maintain good discipline; it helps the student progress in his study in an orderly fashion.

Every student is given a complete checksheet at the start of a course. This is the program to be followed in order to complete the course, and it must not be modified after the course is started. Before the student starts the course, he may add or remove material from the checksheet and so may the school's staff and administration; however, after work starts on it, it must not be modified.

There are four advantages over traditional-style schooling. First, using checksheets enables study at one's own pace; the student can spend more time on items he finds difficult and can quickly get through those items he finds easy. This is very different from the normal system of classroom education, where the teacher/supervisor sets the study speed for the entire class. Second, the system allows misunderstoods and lack of mass to be remedied when they are encountered, not after. Third, the student may, at any point, go back and re-study materials that were not mastered the first time around; in contrast, the traditional system lets a student fail at the end of the course, making him repeat the entire course.

Finally, the whole idea of the academic term becomes redundant; students can be started on a course any time, since they follow the checksheet and study by themselves, not depending on anyone else to set deadlines. Other students, as well as the supervisor, are there to help out, but the idea is that the student follows the recorded materials as they are listed on the checksheet, and that the material is the teacher. The supervisor's job is to keep the classroom free of distractions, to make sure the student studies correctly, and to answer students' questions. If, and only if, he is an expert in the field being studied, the supervisor may also teach in the traditional sense.

## 3.1 Star-Rate Check-Outs

To ascertain the knowledge of a student after he has taken a lesson or read the materials, questions are asked of him in the form of a quiz. In Hubbard's Study Technology, quizzes are also called check-outs.

Because of the higly individualised nature of Hubbard's Study Technology, a standard, written quiz, given to all the students at the same time, is impractical. Instead, the check-out is done orally with visual demonstrations, writing only

## 3.1. STAR-RATE CHECK-OUTS

when needed; the questions are also individualised for each student. Because of the vastly increased workload this entails, the supervisor is no longer the only one entrusted with check-outs. Instead, students are permitted and encouraged to check each other out; it is hoped that they hold sufficient interest in their education to do it faithfully and honestly.

Furthemore, the concept of marking quizzes (with the exceptions of summative assessments and examinations) has been eliminated. Since the goal of study is to learn a workable, applicable technology, knowing 51% of something is useless. A student must fully understand a gradient before he progresses to a new one. If some theory part is not important enough for a 100% pass, only evidence that it has been read is required, and it is not examined at all. They are merely attested on by the student himself. Students attest to having read them, understood them, having cleared any and all misunderstood words, and knowing them well enough to be able to apply them.

To do a checkout the teacher must have read the materials and he must have them in front of him. He asks two kinds of questions: those related to the material as written (theory) and those related to real-life application of the material (practical). He asks the student to demonstrate (more on this later) in clay or on paper, but definitely not with a kit as this method is highly idiosyncratic.

The important points to cover in a theory check-out are: *a)*, the specific rules, natural laws, principles, maxims, or stable data; *b)*, the exact details of how something is done; *c)*, the theory behind why it is done or done that way; and *d)* the definitions of words used. The check-out is geared in the direction of application.

The specific rules, natural laws, principles, maxims, or stable data must be known and the student must be able to demonstrate that their meaning is known to him. Using a demo kit is the normal way to demonstrate. Not knowing the specific rules, natural laws, or principles when the data are put to their final test (applying them in practice) will cause clumsy, robotic, and inept application and frequent mistakes.

The exact details of how something is done must be exactly known, as must be the order in

## 3.1. STAR-RATE CHECK-OUTS

which the steps are taken and a description of the actions, though not *verbatim* (word-for-word). This is usually drilled in Practical before actual application, but the Theory has to be known before practical drilling would make any sense.

The theory behind why it is done, or done in a particular way, must be known; again, this must be given accurately, but not *verbatim*. When doing something in practice, the student will always run into situations that don't seem to match the theory. It is not possible, nor is it practical, to describe (or even attempt to describe) and learn every possible situation beforehand. In practical application, the graduate has to be able to *think with the subject* (this requires affinity), and apply the basic principles and reasoning to the situations he meets.

*Verbatim* answers are only rarely important; in cases where they are required, such as certain mathematical equations which are standardised as being in one particular form, the requirement for *verbatim* answers should be stated clearly on the checksheet. In other cases, giving *verbatim* extracts for answers leads to a perception of arrogance and is irritating to whoever is doing the check-out.

Furthermore, in Hubbard's Study Technology, *verbatim* answers are grounds for a fail, since the goal of study is to encourage critical thinking, and a human tape recorder who simply duplicates what he reads and hears is certainly not thinking critically.

The definitions of words used must also be known. Misunderstoods can prevent understanding completely, and result in misapplication and non-application.

Things to watch out for are incorrect answers, poor or unclear demonstrations, unusually halting speech (this may point to a misanderstood work) and lapses in attention. Any of these recieves an automatic fail, which the couch should deliver by clearly and audibly stating "Fail!" or "Flunk!".

If the student fails, he must re-study the section, paying attention to whatever he failed. He may now get checked out again.

The student is expected to apply the data when needed. This is the purpose of study. To be able to apply the data, rules and laws must be known, details on how to do whatever is to be done must be

## 3.1. STAR-RATE CHECK-OUTS

able to be experienced, the theory behind it must be appreciated, and no misunderstood words must be left behind. Asking for anything above and beyond this is pedantic and will give the student an unnecessary feeling of failure. For instance, *if you checked out a student on Newton's Law of Gravity, you would have him explain the principle, and check his understanding of the formula. You wouldn't check if he knew who Newton was or when he lived.*

When checking out materials, the person doing the check-out (hereafter known as the *teacher*) should do only a *spot check-out*. The teacher should not attempt to cover the full extent of the material. Check-outs are done in the same way as final examinations; only a part of the materials is covered, and if the student has this right, he is assumed to know the rest of it as well.

To be able to do star-rate check-outs on other students, the teacher has to have finished and passed this specific chapter, and he has to have studied the materials he is checking somebody else out in. Ideally, the teacher should be star-rated on those materials, but this is not required. Star-rate check-outs are done by students on each other, and only in exceptional circumstances by the supervisor, unless marked on the checksheet.

Some materials are supervisor check-outs, whether star or zero rated. Such materials include the most important parts of the theory, as well as this chapter (*i.e.,* how to do a star-rate check-out. This is done to get the students started right. The supervisor needs to ensure that his students know how to give standard check-outs by the book. The supervisor also needs to observe his students giving each other check-outs, and assure himself of the quality thereof. If the students are doing it right, their success should not be tampered with in any way. If not, the supervisor should write up what is known as a *pink sheet*: this is a short study order written on a pink sheet of paper. It tells the student to re-study the needed chapters or sections thereof. After the tasks on the pink sheet have been completed, the supervisor checks the student out on this personally.

The remedies for poor quality check-outs are word clearing (to be discussed later in the course pack) and further study of materials. The super-

## 3.1. STAR-RATE CHECK-OUTS 35

visor is *never* to resort to taking over check-outs of all course materials himself; this saps his time, leaving him unable to supervise (per his hat, or job description) effectively.

A general written examination may also be given; final examinations require 85% for a pass. Any wrong answers are handled by having the student re-study and pass a check-out on the pieces missed. This has to be done before he is granted a final pass.

Doing check-outs per above speeds up courses. In addition, it ensures that the important data are known and understood. Good, sound examination is the answer. Irrelevant questions on examinations slow the student down and waste his time. Model kits (the demo kit, the clay demo, and purpose-built models), as well as drawings and diagrams, are to be used extensively. The teacher should ask questions that require an ability to apply; give the student a situation and ask him to tell you how to handle it.

Once again, the important points to cover in a theory check-out are: *a)*, the specific rules, natural laws, principles, maxims, or stable data; *b)*, the exact details of how something is done; c), the theory behind why it is done or done that way; and d) the definitions of words used. The check-out is geared in the direction of application.

The teacher may be arbitrarily strict, according to the importance of the subject, but only as per the four above criteria. If the student does not pass one hundred per cent., the teacher should fail him, give assistance if needed, and re-direct him to the materials. Since the student does one item at a time, it is easy and quick for him to catch up. We don't wait a whole semester, fail the student, and demand that he spends the next five to ten months doing it all again.

# Chapter 4
# The Eight Dynamics

Many philosophers have expounded on the putative goal for humanity; some claim that the goal of humanity is a noble one, such as giving help to those who desire it, whereas others claim that it is a self-serving one, such as pleasure. Both, arguably, are true; yet there is a far more basic goal underlying this, and that is to survive. Biological research is founded upon this goal, and the (valid) assumption that a living being will choose to live rather than to die. Religious works, too, claim this as the most basic goal of Mankind; even psychologist Abraham Maslow placed survival at the base of his *Hierarchy of Human Needs*.

Ron Hubbard subdivided survival into eight instincts or drives that he termed the *Dynamics*; he later added two more to these basic eight, although these two are not widely known. Each person wishes to survive through these drives (whether there are eight, ten, or more is debatable), and he wishes to survive through as many of these at the same time as possible. Whereas the *Hierarchy of Human Needs* is taken as a pyramid, with the most basic goal (survival) larger than the ones above it (safety, belonging, esteem, self-actualisation, and self-transcendence), Hubbard's *Dynamics* are all equal, since any of these can exist before the others are fulfilled. There are two additional dynamics listed here; these are extensions to Hubbard's original philosophy, and have been listed at the end so as not to change the numbering of the other ten.

1. Self;

2. Family (and Friends);

3. Group;

4. Humanity;

5. Life;

6. Universe;

7. Spirit;

8. Allness;

9. Æsthetics;

10. Ethics;

11. Technology;

12. Administration.

The first dynamic relates to one's personal survival as a human being. Anything one does by or for himself in the name of survival is a first-dynamic activity; examples include eating, drinking, reading by oneself. The first dynamic, in other words, is the effort to survive as an individual, to be an individual, to attain the highest level of survival for the longest possible time by oneself.

The second dynamic relates to existence as a future generation, but it also includes one's intimate friends. The human as a sexual being belongs in the second dynamic, but so does his mother, father, sisters, brothers, sons, and daughters. His friends belong in the second dynamic as well.

The third dynamic relates to the urge to survive as part of a group, with the individual furnishing the motivation. All groups, temporary and permanent, political and social, belong in the third dynamic, and each one is a third dynamic. One's classmates, colleagues, countrymen all belong in the third dynamic.

The fourth dynamic relates to survival toward Mankind as a whole. Every human being in the world belongs to the fourth dynamic; whereas the traditional 'races' belong in the third dynamic, the fourth dynamic consists of the one true Race—the Human Race. Doing things 'for Humanity' (relief efforts, or leaving behind a legacy of some sort) exists on the fourth dynamic.

The fifth dynamic relates to survival toward life as a whole. Each and every living thing in the world is part of the fifth dynamic: crickets, whales, birds, and trees all form the fifth dynamic. Man's urge to survive as a part of life as a whole, to keep one's home a welcoming place, as it were, also makes up the fifth dynamic.

The sixth dynamic relates to the Universe and to survival toward all things physically in existence. The innate desire to keep the Universe in existence is the essence of the sixth dynamic; one does not wish to destroy the wider world he lives in, and considers creation and destruction even in this immeasurable context.

The seventh dynamic relates to survival as and toward all things spiritual. Thoughts on ghosts, spirits, and the self as a spiritual being, as well as thoughts on the afterlife, these belong on the seventh dynamic.

The eighth dynamic relates to survival toward a Supreme Being, God, Great Architect of the Universe, or prime mover unmoved. The seventh and eighth dynamics are self-defined and self-discovered; one is encouraged to answer the ultimate questions, such as what lies at the end of his life, and if there is a prime mover unmoved, by himself for his own benefit.

## CHAPTER 4. THE EIGHT DYNAMICS

The ninth dynamic relates to æsthetics—the concept of beauty, and survival toward the concept of æsthetics and as a creative force generally. For instance, one wishes to survive through the creations he leaves behind after his death.

The tenth dynamic relates to ethics and justice, and survival towards and through ethics and justice. Doing good deeds falls under the tenth dynamic; one survives psychologically by being just, fair, ethical, and other such abstract descriptions.

The eleventh dynamic relates to technology, which is defined as a coherent, workable body of knowledge. One survives after his first-dynamic death through his discoveries and the technology these discoveries were moulded into; for example, Freud and Jung, both dead, survive through their respective practices of psychotherapy, which are still used to this day.

The twelfth dynamic relates to administration. This is similar to the third-dynamic groups, except an administration is a body created to oversee the running of a technology. When one discovers a technology, he wishes that this technology will not become lost or corrupted, but only added to, through the years; therefore, he creates an administration to oversee this technology, and the spirit in which his technology is created expresses itself in the administration he devised to oversee it.

Let us take the example of a soldier who jumps on a grenade. Although he is certainly risking first-dynamic death, his platoon (the third dynamic) will survive and be thankful to him for ensuring their survival. If his side wins the war, his family (the second dynamic) will also survive, and—though grieving for their loss—be thankful that the soldier fought and died for freedom. If he believes he is a spiritual being (seventh dynamic) and that he will be judged by God (eighth dynamic) after his death, he may live eternity in paradise for his honourable (tenth dynamic) sacrifice. Furthermore, he may have made some discoveries in peacetime, and he will have left behind these discoveries (eleventh dynamic) and someone to maintain them (twelfth dynamic). Although the action he took may cause his death, or—at the very least—loss of limbs, he will certainly survive in other ways.

The student should make good choices in school and in life; it is preferable to work on two dynamics, rather than just one, and it is preferable to work on three, rather than two. In this way, the student gains responsibility for more than just himself, which is a good thing, especially if he later works in a field where *esprit de corps* is essential.

# Chapter 5

# Twinning

In teaching or learning a subject (sometimes these two are one and the same), it is expedient to assign each student a *twin*. *Twinning* is defined as the pairing up of two students training on the same subject to work together on their materials. Some classes twin only some of the time; whether they call it twinning, pairing up, or getting into groups, that's what it is. However, twinning should be employed wherever it seems to be useful, because it probably will be.

Twinning is mandatory on those courses where

the essence of the course is to train the student in the practical application of the data. Even though such courses also include theory, the final objective of such a course is a person trained and drilled in the doingness involved and twinning is absolutely essential for this purpose.

Thus, on such a course, twins are assigned at the beginning of the course and they remain assigned through to the completion of that course. This is called "assigning twins in concrete". One does not musical chair twins, once assigned, nor allow them to drift from one twin to another.

The whole essence of twinning is to get two students to work together, to assist each other and take responsibility for getting each other successfully through the course.

*The rule of twinning is that is is done on a* **turn-about** *basis.* Turn-about is done as follows:

One student coaches his twin through a drill or a section of a drill. They then turn-about and the second twin does the same drill or section of that drill, in addition to the next drill or next section of the drill. They then turn-about again, with the first student doing the drill his twin has just done, again in addition to the one following.

With the turn-about system, one person is not constantly leading, and misunderstoods are kept picked up between twins. The twins keep apace with each other, there are no imbalances in roles, and both students are kept progressing.

*A twin is responsible for assuring himself that the student with whom he is twinned knows, and can apply, the material he has studied.* Twins must be made aware of this responsibility at the onset of the course.

The twin *word-clears* (more on this later) his fellow student. He listens to his sentences and sees that they are correct and fit the definition of the word being cleared. He makes sure his twin understands the materials. If the student doesn't know them cold, the twin helps the student find his misunderstood words and gets him through any difficulties.

If a student 'flunks' (fails) a teacher check-out on materials he's been passed on by his twin, both students fail; this is called a double flunk. The idea of this is to make both twins accountable for each other's knowledge.

# CHAPTER 5. TWINNING

It is the teacher-supervisor's responsibility to enforce the rules of twinning. He assigns twins, pairing them according to their capabilities; he ensures twinning is being done by the book, on a turn-about basis, with *both* students making progress. He makes sure twins are wearing their hats (doing their jobs, in other words) as twins and taking responsibility for getting each other through, exactly as laid out in course materials.

When twinning is done correctly, hardly anything can go wrong. The only possible problems are if a student, for one reason or another, leaves the course, or if there is an odd number of students to begin with. What happens to the student left over? If the situation is not handled, the student may not even be capable of completing the course.

The usual thing to do in this situation is to match the remaining student up with a set of twins of comparable ability and advancement, and turn the partnership into a trio. Once formed, the trio is run as tightly as any twinship would be, although the turn-about system must be adjusted to a round robin. For example, Alice coaches (teaches) Bob,

Bob coaches Charlie, Charlie coaches Alice.

One of the reasons twinning is important is that it brings a student into the third, or group, dynamic. A student working by himself is on the first dynamic—the self. It is far easier to work on the third dynamic—the group dynamic. Putting students onto the third dynamic puts them into communication, into action, and into participation. Twinning gets students extroverted; it also gets them to take some responsibility for their fellow Man.

Another reason why twinning is important is for the psychological well-being of the student. This is because a person being trained is mainly working on an inflow basis; he is predominantly listening and reading, which means that information is flowing in, rather than out. Day after day, it is inflow, inflow, inflow, and this tends to put him at effect. In other words, the one-way transfer of information can cause the student to feel as if he is not in control of (what Hubbard called at cause over) himself. To put himself at cause, the student must balance his inflow with outflow. The balance is what keeps him in control.

# CHAPTER 5. TWINNING

To apply knowledge or skills, a person must satisfy himself that he is at cause over the knowledge he holds. When he is not trained to be in control, a "stuck flow" phenomenon can result. What this means is that he can not reliably outflow the information. Outflow can take many forms, but it is most acutely related to teaching and to doing, or to broadcasting information. If he ever needs to apply the information he is learning, he will need to learn to outflow it, and education as currently done does not concentrate enough on the outflow.

Twinning has the virtue of balancing inflow and outflow. It will be found that when the person comes to apply the technology, that is, the practice of the thing rather than the theory, he is already able to outflow if he was trained using twinning.

# Chapter 6

# Building Understanding

In learning material, whether through a course, on one's own, or with a study partner, the learner seeks understanding of the subject; when applying this material, he is expressing this understanding. In addition, the relationships that form between the student—or students—and those around him, are built on this same concept. Finally, people try to understand themselves, and others, every day of their lives.

## CHAPTER 6. BUILDING UNDERSTANDING

The best definition of understanding is one given in a First Edition of *Webster's Dictionary of Synonyms*, 1942:

> *Understand.* To have a clear and true idea or conception, or full and exact knowledge, of something. In general it may be said that *understand* refers to the result of a mental process or processes (a clear and exact idea or notion, or full knowledge). *Understand* implies the power to receive and register a clear and true impression.

What this definition does not say, however, is that understanding is built in the manner of an equilateral triangle, and that this triangle is made of *affinity*, *reality*, and *communications*. When one of the sides is cut out, the triangle collapses in what is termed an *A.R.C. break*. When one of the sides becomes longer (greater), the triangle as a whole becomes bigger, leading to greater understanding. This triangle is called the A.R.C. triangle, after its individual components.

Affinity is the love or liking for something, or someone, and is thought to involve the consideration of distance. The greatest affinity for someone would involve the active desire to occupy the same space as him; if one feels zero affinity (this is known as apathy or ambivalence), he feels comfortable at any distance from the subject. Conversely, if one has negative affinity (this is known as antipathy or hate) for someone, he usually tries to put some distance between them. The goal is for the student to have greater affinity for people, objects, and concepts—for him to like and respect them, rather than to be angered and frustrated by them.

One also has a total amount of affinity in general—his "mental space", so to speak. Someone with a lot of total affinity finds it easy to include a lot of people and things in this space; he sees other viewpoints, as well as his own. He is able to, as the Native American adage states, "walk a mile in another man's moccasins". In more technical terms, the student can assume the *beingness* of another; this need not refer to people only, but also to every other thing, living, dead, or inanimate. A good

## 54 CHAPTER 6. BUILDING UNDERSTANDING

pilot, for instance, can be the helicopter; its controls become an extension of his arms and legs, its engine, a surrogate for his beating heart.

Although it was stated above that affinity involves loving or liking someone or something, this is something of an over-simplification. Antipathy can sometimes, if supported by communication of some sort and a common agreement on something, turn into affinity. This is best explained by a physical fight; two people who hate each other, for one brief moment in time, can stand to be close to one another, even if just for the single purpose of throwing punches.

Reality is a matter of shared agreement, or commonality; if two people see things in the same way, they have a common reality. The term *reality*, as used here, however, is not to be confused with the idea of objective reality (i.e. fact as opposed to fantasy); reality, in the context of the A.R.C. triangle, is certainly observable, but not objective. Each observer of a situation creates his own mental picture thereof. Not only is he standing in a different location, and thus sees the object from a different angle, but he also sees things through the filter of his own attitudes and considerations.

Sharing a reality simply means agreement in mutual subjective understanding of the world; our understanding of the world comes through our senses, and so our understanding of the world might not reflect what is actually going on. A blind man has a very different reality to that of a deaf man, for example. Each person has his own reality, his own manner of understanding of the world. For understanding to occur, two entities must have some common ground between their realities.

High reality between two people need not mean that they fully agree on what they are talking about; if they totally agreed, there would be no point in talking about it anyway. It simply means that they agree on the context; they are willing to explore each other's ideas. Two physicists share a reality; although they may have different opinions, they can discuss physical phenomena within the same frame of reference. However, if a ballerina joined in on the discussion, she would not necessarily have the same reality, and the talk might bore her.

Realities at odds with each other need not be so dramatic and obvious; a married couple arguing

## CHAPTER 6. BUILDING UNDERSTANDING

also has reality issues. He may see reality as a controlling wife dictating his every move, while she may see reality as an uncaring husband married more to his job than to her, who comes and goes with no warning or consideration. There can be no agreement until each side accepts at least some aspect of the other's perception of reality.

Often, one's reality changes, or is made to change by another; changes in reality can be brought about temporarily through the use of drugs or hypnosis, or permanently through verbal abuse and physical violence. An individual's own reality can be beaten out of him, so he agrees with the agressor; they will share a reality simply because the individual wishes to live. In this way, human robots are made by oppressive governments.

The third and last factor is communication; this is the most straight-forward aspect of the A.R.C. triangle. Communication, quite simply, is the exchange of information; without communication, there can be no increase in understanding, no formation of affinity, and no understanding of another's reality. One can not talk adequately to a man if he is sub-apathetic to him; in fact, one would not talk to him at all. It is possible to communicate with inanimate objects as well; simply touching a brick wall is communication, even though no real exchange of ideas is taking place.

The inter-relationship of this triangle becomes apparent at once when one is asked, "Have you ever tried to talk to an angry man?" Without a high degree of liking, and without some basis of agreement, there is no communication. Without communication and some basis of emotional response, there can be no reality. Without some basis for agreement and communication, there can be no affinity.

The A.R.C. triangle applies to everyday life as well as study; in fact, it is the cornerstone of all human relationships, as well as the relationships humans have with animals and with inanimate objects.

For instance, if a man meets another man on a business trip and begins talking to him about music, this is *communication*. They come to an agreement that popular music bands of the 2000s are mass-manufactured and worthless—they share

## 58 CHAPTER 6. BUILDING UNDERSTANDING

a *reality*. The two men trade telephone numbers and become friends shortly after, as a product of *affinity*.

Another example is of a master mechanic. He has repaired motors of all kinds for years; just by listening to the motor, he can tell precisely what is wrong with it, and he knows where to look. He has read all the relevant literature, which has *communicated* knowledge to him; he has a lot of experience, which has given him a foothold in *reality*; and, because of his high *affinity*, he is capable of *being* the motor. He is in pain when he hears the gears grind, and he feels good when he sees that the motor is purring like a big cat. Because affinity, reality, and communication for motors are all there in spades, the mechanic can be said to understand motors. Even though motors are not living things, it is certainly possible to develop a shared *beingness* with motors, as the mechanic has done.

Good affinity, reality, and communication need not be positive, however; two men in a drunken brawl certainly share good A.R.C., and understand each other, yet the resulting fistfight can hardly be said to be a positive thing. The reason they can be said to understand each other is simple: they are close to each other, and thus have a mutual *affinity*; they have a shared *reality* about fighting; and the insults, kicks, punches, and objects thrown at each other make for good *communication*.

Similarly, two patients in the psychiatric ward of the local hospital may be in good A.R.C. and be said to understand each other, yet clearly be insane. For instance, they may share the *reality* that evil Martians have landed on the driveway; they may be *communicating* at great length about it; and they may be friends and thus share an *affinity* towards each other. The reason they are deemed insane, in spite of their mutual understanding, is because they share a reality that is not supported by society; everyone else who looks at the driveway sees nothing but two ambulances and a police car.

# Chapter 7

# Glibness in the Student

In the traditional classroom system of education, the circumstances align in such a way as to prefer a student who will not make it in the application of the subject at hand in the field. The reason for this is that theory trumps heavily over practice in this system, and this tends to lead to the student who is extraordinarily talented at setting up a tape recorder in his mind, but not much else. A *glib* student such as this will get high marks on tests and

## 62 CHAPTER 7. GLIBNESS IN THE STUDENT

examinations, will duplicate materials very well (almost to perfection), but will not translate the materials he has read and duplicated into application in the physical world.

A glib student is generally *rewarded* in academic studies with high marks, but, unfortunately, the real test comes in the world of work, at which time it is far too late. The glib student has developed ways of loading study materials into his mind and of giving them back on demand; he is unable, however, to get conceptual understanding and application of what he has studied. In traditional academic study, glibness tends to be the norm and not the exception.

This approach is clearly wrong. The goal of nearly any sort of study is to apply it in some way; even pure mathematics contains an element of application. Glibness must be found and broken through before the student can begin to study; this is done by asking for demonstration or application. When asked to demonstrate or do something with a principle, the glib student will hesitate, make mistakes, refuse, or complain. The glib student can be saved by consistently and frequently requesting demonstration and application of what is being studied.

There is a communication lag when anyone is asked a question; a comm lag is the time between the end of the question and the start of the answer. A glib student will have a short comm lag when asked a theoretical question, but a long comm lag when asked to perform a practical exercise or to demonstrate. An actually good student will have short comm lags across the board.

# Chapter 8
# Confusions

In Study Technology, the word *confusion* is used in two different ways: as an uncountable[1] noun, it refers to the state of mind of a student who is overwhelmed by the subject he is studying, and as a countable[2] noun, it refers to a collection of data or particles in unpredictable, random motion. This chapter concentrates mainly on the second meaning of the word. The term *particle* is used

---
[1] simply *confusion*
[2] *a confusion*

loosely in this definition; it refers to the smallest component part of any situation.

An example of a confusion is a busy call centre; the operator looks at the switchboard, sees all fifty lights blinking, and may be mentally paralysed, not knowing which button to press, as a result of the information that is overwhelming him. Another would be an unsupervised classroom; students yelling, throwing paper aëroplanes around, and generally mis-behaving would overwhelm a new teacher on his first day, possibly to the point of mental paralysis. The scene of a major accident would also be a confusion to the uninitiated; however, those who work in emergency services *must* know how to handle the confusion—otherwise, loss of life would surely result.

There is a simple reason why confusions are confusing, and there is a simple way to resolve confusions. By definition, confusions lack stable data; the data-points or particles are, in absolutistic terms, all moving in random directions. Therefore, the solution to most any problem with an element of confusion is to consider it in relativistic terms—to *pick a stable datum*. At work, a phrase one may hear is to "pick a fire and put it out"; this is the best possible advice one may be given for any such situation.

For instance, the confused telephone operator, upon seeing the switchboard, makes a decision, correctly or incorrectly, to take a certain call first. He can now visualise the calls relatively to the first call he answered, which can clear up a lot of the negative mental feelings (predominantly anxiety) that can pop up when entering a confusion. The teacher, too, simply has to choose the first student to discipline; after that, a plan more easily forms in his mind. Because of the risk of death were one to choose incorrectly, there is a well-established system for handling confusions at major accident scenes and in hospital; it is called *triage*. Emergency workers sort casualties into three groups (excluding deaths): life-threatening injuries; serious injuries; and minor injuries. Categorising injuries in this manner allows the workers to find out who to evacuate first.

Confusion is also inherent in study. Any new subject can feel confusing at first; this happens because the student has not formed any stable data

# CHAPTER 8. CONFUSIONS

about the subject. As the student builds up his stable data, his ability to handle confusions in the subject increases. However, it is wise to evaluate one's data before one accepts them as stable; authors of books are rarely unerring, and never neutral. A datum that one has accepted as stable might well turn out to be a mistake on the part of the author, or, even worse, a deliberate untruth. Ideal stable data are the actual basic axioms and principles that a subject is built on.

If one's stable data are shaken, the confusion will return until he has reëstablished his data or found new ones. For instance, if one bases his study of aëroplanes on the datum that they fly because they have engines and propellers, he might get confused if he is shown a glider.

There are two possible reasons, then, for running into a confusion in study: first, one might have gone too fast into a subject he did not have enough stable data on; and second, some of his existing data might have been shaken. Sometimes, one will be forced to re-evaluate existing stable data; although this may not be comfortable, it is necessary if one has chosen inaccurate or false data.

Changing stable data might feel like taking a step back, but it is always followed by at least two steps forward.

# Chapter 9
# Relaxation and Study

A high-pressure environment is rarely conducive to study; even when the subject itself is practiced in a high-pressure environment, its study should not be performed like this. For instance, a medical school need not subject its students to on-the-job pressures so they learn better. Similarly, the success of study has nothing to do with how many pages the student has read, or how much one has worked on learning something. All that counts is how well the student can apply what he has learned.

## CHAPTER 9. RELAXATION AND STUDY

There are factors that will increase the degree of learning without increasing the amount of hard work; as a matter of fact, learning is better the less hard it is. A student will learn better if he is attentive, but relaxed; the more stressed he is, the less effective his learning will be. The best student is one who is well-fed and well-rested, who currently is physically relaxed, who is in a pleasant environment, and who is presented with material in a non-stressful manner.

To learn quickly, one does not need his mind working at a very high speed; quite the opposite, in fact. One would learn better by relaxing with the material. Genius-level thinkers, as well as exceptionally-fast learners, often do not increase their mental activity when they learn or solve problems; rather, they relax more, both mentally and physically, when they are presented with a problem to solve.

When the student has an urgent need to learn something, he should not pressure himself through it in a stressful manner. Rather, he should ensure he is relaxed and comfortable, and that his daily worries are out of the way. The student should relax physically and mentally, remember the salient points of Study Technology, and work *with* the material. Relaxation does not mean being sleepy or absent-minded; attentive relaxation—awareness, but not under pressure—is required here.

# Chapter 10

# The Pyramid of Knowledge

Knowledge in any subject can be described as a pyramid of hierarchically related data. The top of the pyramid contains the simplest, most general, most wide-ranging, most abstract data in the subject; the further down one goes in the pyramid, the more specific, complex, limited, and practical the data gets. The general principles at the top can be explored and illustrated by the manifestations and examples found further down. Any conflict between specifics low in the pyramid are resolved by moving one or more steps up and inspecting the general principles the specifics are based on.

The process of developing lower parts of the pyramid is called deduction. It is the construction of specifics by the application of general rules. General laws can be combined logically to establish and predict practical data. Engineering is an example of this. The mathematical formulæ for the construction of bridges are well-known—they simply need to be applied to the situations and conditions at hand.

The process of building the top parts up from the bottom parts is known as induction. One can guess at theories that will explain the maximum number of observed specifics. The theory or fact that explains the most is the best candidate for a high position. Science usually uses this approach; Darwin's theories on evolution and survival of the fittest came about through inductive logic. In induction, a theory is brought up, and then one checks if reality and theory match.

All subjects possess a pyramid of knowledge, whether they are presented as such or not. It is the duty of the student in the field to structure his own understanding and to get the relative importances and seniorities right. The higher the datum is in the pyramid of knowledge, the more important it is to know it fully. Lower data can always be developed if the higher are known; it may not be possible, however, to have conceptual understanding of abstract, wide-spanning data, unless a sufficient number of specifics and examples have been understood and evaluated.

# Chapter 11

# Representation of Concepts

In the words of an old maxim, *a picture is worth a thousand words.* Yet, in truth, the idea need not be represented by the usual definition of a *picture* (a simple sculpture or even an abstract collection of objects will do), and representation is worth far more than a thousand words. In fact, it is, for most subjects, absolutely essential; education without the presence of the object being studied is not only hard *for* the student, but also hard *on* the student. The closer a representation is to the object being studied, the more *mass* it has, and it is also possible to speak of mass–the physical objects of life–in general terms. The ideas conveyed about or through an object are also known as its *significance*.

If one was studying about aircraft, the mass would be an aeroplane. One could read cockpit manuals and listen to lectures for years, but if he had never seen the inside of an aeroplane, all the effort would come to nil, because he is aware of all the theory, the significance, but is unable to apply it since there is no mass.

Because it may be inconvenient to have the actual object being studied in the classroom, tools and techniques have been devised to remedy this. These tools have likely been around since the dawn of time, but they have never before been incorporated into a cohesive theory. In this book, any attempt at bringing mass to the ideas being studied, short of the object itself, will be called a *demonstration*. According to the Collins English Dictionary, a demonstration is defined as "an explanation, display, illustration, or experiment showing how something works"; this is the goal of a demonstration, as used here.

One way of doing a demonstration, or a *demo*, is with a demonstration kit. A demo kit is nothing more or less than a collection of odds and ends, such as push pins, elastic bands, and bottle caps, that can be used to represent whatever he is studying and help him understand its workings. Anything can be demonstrated with the demo kit, some things more successfully than others: ideas, objects, relationships, or how something works can all be demonstrated with this simple model. One simply uses the small objects to represent the relationships between the component parts of the concept. The objects can be moved about to show its mechanics and actions.

Another way of demonstrating something is with a two dimensional representation: a drawing, photograph, or sketch works very well for many things. Someone working at his office desk can take a pencil and paper, and get the mass of whatever he is doing by sketching it out, or by drawing a graph. Solving a mathematical problem also falls into this category, although the 'sketch' is nothing more than abstract representations of quantities. There is a rule, used in architecture and engineering, which states that *if you can not demonstrate something in two dimensions, you have it wrong.* Although this is arbitrary and based on judgement and discretion, it is very workable.

A third method of demonstration is possible. Although this particular method is the most complex, it also provides the most mass, and certain concepts are best represented this way if they can not be brought into the classroom. This method, called a clay demonstration, involves the use of Plasticine and paper labels to model a concept. The purpose of clay demonstration is to make the materials being studied more real to the student and to convey a proper balance of mass and significance.

Any student can use clay to demonstrate actions, objects, definitions, and principles. He sits at a table set up with different colours of Plasticine for his use. In doing a clay demonstration, the student must demonstrate the object or principle and label each of its parts. The clay must adequately represent the mass; it should not amount to labelled balls of clay. Small strips of paper are used for labels. Art, however, is no object in making a clay demo; crude forms will do, as long as they visibly represent the object being studied.

The table used for the demonstration can be of any kind, and the student can stand or sit while working. In situations where nothing else is available, even an upturned orange crate will do. However, the working surface of the clay table must be a smooth surface, such as oilcloth or linoleum; otherwise, the clay will stick to it and the clay leavings will make life difficult for the student. Casters (wheels) may be put on the legs of the clay table, especially where it must be moved a lot.

The amount of each colour is not important as long as there is at least a pound or so of each. Colours are only used to make a student see the difference between one object and another; they need not be realistic. For instance, a human model can be black, white, purple, or green, although one rarely sees a purple person.

At times, the instructor or course supervisor may demonstrate on the clay table before the class. For this reason, it can be of tremendous benefit to have a table that can tilt to a downward angle of approximately thirty degrees. The method of doing this is up to the instructor; although the ideal set-up is a large engineer's drawing table, two equally-sized bricks can be used instead. It is suggested, for ease of use, that a table that tilts in this fashion have a raised lip on the side facing the class. Although clay does not usually slip on linoleum, it is sometimes dropped, and it is easier to retrieve it if it has not dropped to the floor. Furthermore, if the table has a removable covering (a sheet of linoleum or a pane of glass for example), it is not liable to slide off if the table has a guard board.

Everything in a clay demonstration must be labelled, no matter how crudely; scraps of paper or light card will suffice for students. Furthermore, labels should be put on immediately after each component of the demonstration is built; doing all the clay work first, and then all the labels, or vice versa, is liable to result in nothing but confusion.

For instructor use (this includes students demonstrating to the entire class), the best manner to construct labels is to use white index cards inked with a felt-tip pen, and then to tape this to a toothpick or tongue depressor.

Clay demonstrations must be *big*. The purpose of clay demos is to make the material more real to the student; if the demo is small, it may not furnish enough mass to the student. Big clay demos are more successful in increasing student understanding.

Directions of motion or travel are indicated with arrows; these can be made out of clay, or as labels. This is important: lack of clarity about which way what travels can make the demo less understandable. Pure thoughts, or significances, are made by forming a thin-edged ring of clay with a large hole in it (a 'lasso' shape, in other words).

For example, if a student, Alice, wishes to demonstrate herself thinking about holding a ball, she would model the three-dimensional equivalent of a stick drawing and label this *Alice*. She would attach a clay lasso to the top of 'her' head, labelling this *thought*. In the centre of the loop formed by the thought, she would place a second, smaller model of herself, labelling this *Alice*. In the second model's arms, Alice would place a ball, labelling it *ball*.

It is important to note that the clay table is not

just for a few terms; it can be used for all definitions. Anything can be demonstrated in clay, with the ingenuity of the instructor or the student and his understanding of the concepts being demonstrated being the only limits. In fact, the simple process of finding out *how* to demonstrate it can bring about understanding of the mass itself. If one can represent a mass in clay, he understands it; if he can't, he may not understand what it is. Clay and labels work only if the concept is fully understood, and doing a clay demonstration brings out an understanding of them.

Purpose-built kits, too, can be used: ball-and-stick models for chemistry are an invaluable teaching tool and may work better than any of the above. Similarly, algebra tiles can be used to teach mathematics. Like each of the demonstrations above, these have benefits and drawbacks, though. The drawbacks are that a purpose-built demonstration can not be used to demonstrate other things, and also that having many purpose-built kits can be prohibitive in cost, as they sell for far more than 'a bunch of odds and ends' (as the demo kit has been described), or even for variously-coloured blocks of Plasticine.

# Chapter 12
# The Gradient of Study

When studying, especially if studying a practical activity, it will be found that some steps naturally precede others. This is termed a gradient; like a staircase, one must proceed step by step and level by level. Each step, also called a gradient, is easily attainable from the previous one; however, if gradients are skipped, the student runs the risk of tripping over himself.

The responsibility for following the gradient of study rests on the student, as well as on the author of the text under study. The author must clearly mark off the gradients as such; he must include all the gradients; and he must do so in the correct order. The student must follow these gradients when learning the procedure. An analogy may be drawn: the builder of a house must build stairs into a two-floor house, he must build them at a safe slope, and the staircase can not have, say, a six-foot step somewhere in the middle. The occupants of the house are responsible for not taking the stairs two or three at a time, or taking the bannister instead.

Traditional 'confusion' generally results from a skipped gradient; if the student feels that he has somehow tripped over himself, mentally speaking, or if he simply gets lost in a particular step of a procedure, this definitely signals a skipped gradient. For certain practical activities that involve a certain element of risk, such as operating a vehicle (whether human-powered, motorised, wheeled, or airborne), skipping a gradient may also have safety implications. For instance, a young boy learning to ride a bicycle for the first time and not using training wheels will likely fall.

Furthermore, if a student becomes confused at some point in the middle of a procedure, and the problem is traced to a skipped gradient (for instance, if the student complains that he can not make head nor tail of a particular step, although the text is clearly written) the problem shall be found in the step immediately preceding the one that he is apparently having trouble with. The student must be directed to go back over what he understood well, and the problem will most likely be found there. This is known as *cutting back* the gradient.

Again, this problem is most common when the student is engaged in what L.R.H. terms 'doingness': the performance of some action or activity as opposed to academic or intellectual study.

# Chapter 13

# The Misunderstood Word

The final barrier to study is, in contrast to the others, a simple concept to grasp, but often the highest hurdle for the student. The misunderstood word—that is to say, a word which is poorly, partially, or not at all understood—can be a source of many problems, up to and including the complete failure to retain portions of the material being taught. The term *word* is here, and shall continue to be, used *loosely*; a *misunderstood*, as it is sometimes called, can in fact be any semantically meaningful construction, or what linguists call a *morpheme*.

A misunderstood is remedied by *word clearing*: this is also called looking it up in a dictionary. A dictionary is a book (or, in this modern age, a computer file) containing the words of a language or subject, usually arranged in alphabetical order, which gives information about their meanings and pronunciations. Dictionaries are vital tools in studying any subject; however, they vary in gradient and in accuracy, and the wrong dictionary can actually confuse a student. Because this is a common problem, and because different dictionaries define words in different ways, there should always be an abundance of dictionaries in the classroom.

The usual symptom of a misunderstood is a loss of attention, blank in memory, or 'dozing off' immediately following the word in question. These symptoms can sometimes be traced to an organic cause; for example, the student may not have had enough sleep prior to course, or he may have a physical (*e.g.*, narcolepsy) or mental (*e.g.*, attention deficit disorder) condition that may influence his thought patterns. In this case, the organic cause is most likely; however, where an organic cause is non-existent, a misunderstood is usually the problem.

Using the wrong dictionary can make learning much harder for a student, wasting his time and money. If a student finds he is getting into word chains (looking up misunderstoods that appear in the definitions of other misunde4stoods), this might be a sign of a dictionary that is too far up the gradient (is *out-gradient*). Unabridged and college dictionaries are often quite technical; young and foreign-language students may not find them to their liking because they will most likely spend too much time chasing around the dictionary clearing up word chains. Other students, meanwhile, may love the college dictionaries and would find the additional data helpful.

Consider this: a simple child's dictionary may define 'bird' in this way: 'an animal covered with feathers that has two legs and lays eggs'. Now, this same word in a hypothetical college dictionary would be, 'any oviparous, bipedal, warm-blooded vertebrate of the class Aves, having a feathered body and forelimbs modified into wings'. This would most likely lead such a student into definitions of 'oviparous', 'bipedal', 'vertebrate', 'Aves', 'forelimbs', and 'modified'. After a bit of this, the student will have looked up a large number of words that he has never heard before, and he will be growing steadily more frustrated. The solution is to replace his college dictionary with a child's one, and he will make progress.

As students' vocabulary increases and they become more literate, each will, in time, graduate to a more advanced dictionary. As students progress through their courses, they will, more often than not, switch from a beginners' dictionary to a college dictionary, and, sooner or later, to the Oxford English Dictionary. Some students use two or more dictionaries, switching between one for general use and one for advanced words or technical jargon. In some professions, this becomes, more or less, mandatory; no general English dictionary will define the word 'mortmain', but Black's Law Dictionary does: 'A term applied to denote the alienation of lands or tenements to any corporation, sole or aggregate, ecclesiastical or temporal.' An English lawyer will most probably have no problem defining 'tenements', 'corporate', 'aggregate', 'ecclesiastical', and 'temporal', but a beginning student, again, might.

Although a number of dictionaries are suggested and endorsed by the authors of this book, students may elect to use a different dictionary, with one caveat: *dinky* dictionaries are not recommended. The slang word 'dinky' is defined by the Funk & Wagnalls College Dictionary as 'small; insignificant'; a dinky dictionary, then, is a small dictionary that provides definitions inadequate for full conceptual understanding of a word. In the category of dinky dictionaries fall most *pocket*, *compact*, and *little* dictionaries; they are the paperback sort that fits in your pocket, and are usually found at magazine counters at chemists and supermarkets.

> In learning the meaning of words, small dictionaries are very often a greater liability than they are a help. The meanings they give are often circular, like 'CAT: An animal.' 'ANIMAL: A

cat.' They do not give enough meaning to escape the circle. The meanings given are often inadequate to get a real concept of the word. The words are too few and even common words are often missing. [...]

Little pocket book dictionaries may have their uses for travelling and reading newspapers, but they do get people in trouble. I have seen people find a word in them and then look around in total confusion. For the dinky dictionary did not give the full meaning or the second meaning they really needed.

**So the dinky dictionary may fit in your pocket, but not in your mind.** (L. R. H.)

The human factor is prone to error, and dictionaries are no exception. It has been found that some dictionaries have left out definitions, or worse, contain misleading, incomplete, or false definitions. If, when using a dictionary, a student encounters what he feels is a false definition, this can be handled in the following manner. First, the student must assure himself that there are no misunderstoods in the definition in question; then, he should consult another dictionary and check its definition for the word being cleared. For accuracy, a third dictionary should be used. Similar steps should be taken if a student runs into, or believes he has run into, an omitted definition.

When clearing definitions in a dictionary, the student must also take care to clear the *derivation* of the word. A word's derivation, also called its *etymology*, is a statement of its origin. Words *originated* somewhere and meant something originally; throughout the ages, though, meanings may have been added, removed, or changed.

Derivations are important in getting a full understanding of the words; by understanding the origin of a word, one will find that he has been greatly assisted in conceptually comprehending a word, which leads to greater comprehension of other words that are derived from the same source.

In spite of the importance of word derivations, it will be often found that a student is ignorant of what a derivation is, or is unable to read the derivations in most dictionaries. For instance, students fail to grasp, until they are told otherwise, that a word in the derivation that is set in capitals generally means that it is fully defined elsewhere in the dictionary. This is one of the two reasons students can have a problem with derivations; the other is that a word or symbol within the derivation is misunderstood.

A sample derivation would be as follows: **THERMOMETER** From Gr. *thermē*, temperature, and L. *metrum* via Gr. *metron*, to measure.

A good dictionary of derivations is *The Oxford Dictionary of English Etymology*, printed by the Oxford University Press.

Finally, when clearing a word, it will be found that some words have definitions that are marked as technical, specialised, obsolete, unique to a particular science or field of study, or simply are obviously not pertinent to the word as used in context. The logical question that should come up in this situation is whether each definition of the word needs to be cleared, and, if not, exactly *what* needs to be cleared.

There is no reason to look up every definition, or even to read specialised definitions for a word. The rule is to know the definition of the word as given for the context in which it is used; the student must look over a full definition to find out which one applies to the text he has been reading, and then clear only that one. Furthermore, the student is not required to clear every word in the definition, only those, if indeed there are any, that he does not understand.

In clearing a word, the student must endeavour to use it in sentences until he has it as a concept. A cleared word has been defined as *a word which has been cleared to the point of full conceptual understanding.*

Although the word *understanding* is a common one, hardly any dictionary has a full and complete definition of it; the sole exception seems to be in a first edition of *Webster's Dictionary of Synonyms*, 1942.

> *Understand.* To have a clear and true idea or conception, or full and exact knowledge, of something. In general it

## 102 CHAPTER 13. MISUNDERSTOODS

may be said that *understand* refers to the result of a mental process or processes (a clear and exact idea or notion, or full knowledge). *Understand* implies the power to receive and register a clear and true impression.

sectionEnglish Dialects
Although the United States of America (for convenience, known hereafter simply as *the U.S.A.*), as well as Great Britain, speak the same language, certain words differ in usage to the point that they may have contradicting meanings 'across the pond'. This was noted even by Irish author George Bernard Shaw, who once wrote that Great Britain and the U.S.A. are "two nations divided by a common language"; his fellow countryman, Oscar Wilde, agreed, stating that Great Britain has "really everything in common with America nowadays, except, of course, language."

Most other English-speaking countries, including Canada, South Africa, Australia, New Zealand, and India, use the British standard; the exceptions include Belize, Puerto Rico, the Philippines, and

Samoa—all areas with American-style vocabulary. The British standard does somewhat vary among writers, as some prefer 'Oxford style' spelling (for instance, mechanize, pasteurize, privatize, tenderize) and others prefer the 'Latinate style' (for instance, mechanise, pasteurise, privatise, tenderise).

However, the major issue here is of vocabulary, rather than spelling. There are certain terms which are used in the British version of English and either not understood or understood in a different way by Americans. This can lead to A.R.C. breaks (specifically, the shared reality breaks down), which can cause arguments, injuries, or even death. A simple example of this is the word *toilet*. In both systems, this word means the act of washing oneself, as well as a receptacle for disposal of bodily wastes; in Great Britain, this word additionally means the room in which this receptacle is contained. An American would probably understand, but never use, the word *toilet* in that context; he would say *restroom* instead.

A misunderstanding there would not cause major problems—maybe a blank look from the hotel receptionist, but not much else. There are cases, however, where a misunderstanding like this would cause injury or death. Consider the word *pavement*; an American understands this to mean a hard, paved surface upon which traffic circulates, while an Englishman understands it to mean the boardwalk or footpath at the side of such a surface—an American would call this a *sidewalk*.

Say a Londoner goes to New York on holiday. He is walking on the pedestrian footpath; suddenly, he hears the loud noise of a steam-roller behind him, as well as a New Yorker shouting "Clear the pavement!" The Londoner understands this to mean to get off the paved footpath, steps onto the roadway, gets run down, and suffers severe injuries as a result.

If this man were to look the definition of *pavement* up in an American dictionary, he'd see that it meant something other than what he believed it to mean, and that the word for the surface he was walking on was *sidewalk*. Most British dictionaries, on the other hand, have no definition for *sidewalk*; those that do would prefix it with the disclaimer *Chiefly Am.* or *Am. usage*.

It is important, therefore, to consult a dictionary appropriate to one's country of residence. If one uses a dictionary that uses a different national standard, he should be aware of this and look up nationally-specific words in a different dictionary to get both meanings.

## 13.1 Types of Misunderstoods

A *false definition* is one that has no relationship to the true meaning of the word. For instance, a person who reads the word 'cat' and believes it means 'box' is labouring under a false definition. Similarly, this is also true of one who sees an equals sign and thinks that it means to subtract twice.

An *incorrect definition* is one that has some relationship to, or is in the same category as, the true meaning of the word. For instance, someone who hears the word 'computer' and believes it means 'typewriter'. This is an incorrect meaning for 'computer', although it is true that typewriters and computers are both machines for word processing. Another example would be a man who sees a full stop after an abbreviation, and halts in

## CHAPTER 13. MISUNDERSTOODS

reading at that point.

An *incomplete definition* is one that only partially covers the true meaning of the word. For instance, someone who reads the word 'office' and believes that it means 'place'. The full definition of the word 'office', as defined in Funk and Wagnalls Standard College Dictionary, is 'A place in which the business of an individual, corporation, government bureau, &c. is carried out; also, the staff and administrative officials working in such a place.' Similarly, a person who knows that an apostrophe denotes the possessive (*i.e.*, that something is owned) but not that it can also denote a contraction (*i.e.*, that letters have been left out) sees the word 'gov't' and tries to find out who gov is.

An *unsuitable definition* is one that does not fit the word as used in context. An example would be someone who reads about 'dressing a turkey' and knows that 'dressing' means 'putting clothes on', and so thinks that clothes are being put on a turkey. 'Dressing' indeed does mean 'to put clothes on'; it also, however, means 'to prepare (fowl, game, fish, &c.) for cooking' (as defined in Funk and Wagnalls Standard College Dictionary)

## 13.1. TYPES OF MISUNDERSTOODS

and that is the definition being used here. Similarly, a person who sees a dash in the sentence 'Read pages 10–20 of *How to Train Your Dragon*' and thinks that it is a minus sign, then can not understand it because he realises you can not subtract twenty from ten, is using an unsuitable definition.

A *homophonic definition* is one which relies on the wrong meaning of a homophone (also known as a homonym). A homophone is a word which has two completely different meanings, and sometimes two different spellings, but is pronounced the same in both cases. For instance, someone who reads the sentence, 'I like to box', and understands this to mean that the writer likes to put things in containers, has the right meaning for the word 'box', but the wrong *word*! The correct definition of the word 'box', as used, is 'to fight another in a boxing match'.

A *substitute definition* occurs when one uses a synonym—a word which has a similar, but not the same, meaning—for the definition of a word. A synonym is not a definition. A synonym is a word having a meaning akin to that of another word. Knowing synonyms for words increases one's vocabulary, but it does *not* show understanding of the meaning of a word. It is advisable to learn the full *definition* of a word as well as its *synonyms*.

For example, a student reads the line, 'The size was Gargantuan', believes he does not understand it, and he looks it up in a dictionary. He finds the definition, 'Suggestive of Gargantua; huge.' He uses 'huge' as a synonym and reads the text line, 'The size was huge.' However, this is wrong. 'Huge' is not 'Gargantuan'. These are synonyms. The sentence is, 'The size was Gargantuan.' The sentence is *not*, 'The size was huge.' The correct procedure is to look it up and *understand* the word that was used. Who was Gargantua? The dictionary says it was the name of a gigantic King in a book by French author Rabelais. No, the sentence was *not* 'The size was a gigantic king'. Instead, the student should make up a few sentences that use the word 'Gargantuan'. In time, he should grow to understand *the* word that was used. Now, what does the sentence 'The size was Gargantuan' mean? It means 'The size was Gargantuan', and *nothing* else.

An *omitted definition* is one that is missing or has been omitted from the dictionary the student

## 13.1. TYPES OF MISUNDERSTOODS    109

is using. For instance, a person hears the line, 'The food here is too rich'. He knows two definitions of the word 'rich': first, 'having large possessions, as of money, goods, or lands; wealthy; opulent', and second, 'of a fuel-air mixture, containing a relatively high ratio of fuel to air'. He can not imagine what food could have to do with fuel-air mixtures or with money. His problem may stem from using a vest-pocket dictionary; 'dinky' dictionaries may not supply the definition he needs, which happens to be: 'having in a high degree qualities pleasing to the senses; luscious to the taste: often implying an unwholesome excess of butter, fats, flavouring, &c.'

Similarly, a person who reads 'He estimated the light at $f$ 5.6' can't figure out what 'f' stands for, so he pulls out his *American Heritage Dictionary* and wonders if it means degrees Fahrenheit, Swiss francs, or sports for 'foul'. Omitted in the American Heritage is the photographic definition of 'f', which simply means 'the number which shows the width of the hole the light goes through in the lens'. One should always have enough dictionaries around, and one is rarely, if ever, enough.

# CHAPTER 13. MISUNDERSTOODS

A *non-definition* is a word which, quite simply, is *not understood*. For instance, a student who reads "The business produced no lucre", and has no definition for 'lucre', will not understand the sentence. The word means 'money, especially as the object of greed; gain.' The student does not have an incorrect, unsuitable, or any other kind of misunderstood; he has a non-understood. The solution in this case is to get a dictionary and to get it properly understood.

## 13.2 Suggested Dictionaries

The following dictionaries have been recommended because they have been found to be better, more accurate, and more useful than others. No one dictionary was found that would be ideal for all students; the choice of dictionary is a matter of personal preference and is dependent on vocabulary and level of literacy.

*Webster's New World Dictionary for Young Readers* is a very simple American dictionary. It is available in most bookstores and is published

## 13.2. SUGGESTED DICTIONARIES

by John Wiley and Sons. It is a hardbound volume, and does not contain derivations; therefore, when using this dictionary, a student must be sure to clear the derivations in a larger dictionary. The definitions in this dictionary are quite good.

*Oxford American Dictionary* is a very good American dictionary, simpler than the college dictionaries, yet more advanced than the beginner's dictionary listed above. It does not list derivations of the words. It is quite an excellent dictionary and very popular with students who want to use an intermediate dictionary. It is published by Oxford University Press.

*Webster's New World Dictionary of the American Language, Student Edition* is an intermediate-level American dictionary which includes derivations. It is published by John Wiley and Sons, and is available in most bookstores.

*The Random House College Dictionary* is somewhat higher of gradient than the dictionaries previously listed; it is a one-volume American college dictionary published by Random House. This Random House dictionary contains a large number of slang definitions and idioms; it also gives good derivations.

*The Webster's New World Dictionary of the American Language, College Edition* is an American college dictionary published by John Wiley and Sons. It is a one-volume dictionary and gives most of the slang definitions and idioms, with good derivations.

*The Concise Oxford Dictionary* is a very concise (hence its name) English dictionary. It is a small, one-volume dictionary. It uses a lot of abbreviations which may take some getting used to, but once the abbreviations are mastered, students find this dictionary as easy to use as any other similarly advanced dictionary. It is less complicated in its definitions than the usual college dictionary, and it has the added benefit that the definitions given are well stated—in other words, it does not give the same definition reworded into several different definitions, the way some dictionaries do. It is printed in Great Britain and the United States by the Oxford University Press.

*The Chambers Dictionary* is an English dictionary printed in Edinburgh, Scotland. Much loved by crossword solvers and Scrabble players, it is

## 13.2. SUGGESTED DICTIONARIES 113

quite thorough, with a focus on dialectal, archaic, eccentric, and unconventional words, but also containing most of the more standard English idioms and slang. *Chambers* is also noted for its dryly jocular definitions, being reminiscent of Johnson's Dictionary in this respect. It is a fairly high-gradient dictionary, however, and is recommended for the more literate students. The definitions are quite thorough, but few examples are given.

Although out of print, the *Funk and Wagnalls New Comprehensive Dictionary of the English Language, International Edition* is one of the most grammatically correct dictionaries there is, and it is probably the best American dictionary available. It was previously published as the *Britannica World Language Edition of Funk and Wagnalls Standard Dictionary* by Encyclopaedia Britannica, Inc., Chicago, and as the *Funk and Wagnalls Standard Dictionary of the English Language, International Edition* by the J. G. Ferguson Publishing Co., Chicago. A college version of this dictionary is also available, as the *Funk and Wagnalls Standard College Dictionary*.

*The Shorter Oxford English Dictionary* is a

## 114 CHAPTER 13. MISUNDERSTOODS

two-volume English dictionary and is a shorter version of The Oxford English Dictionary. It is quite up-to-date and is an ideal dictionary for fairly literate students. Even if not used regularly, it makes a very good reference dictionary. The definitions given in the Oxford dictionaries are usually more accurate and give a better idea of the meaning of the word than any other dictionary. This dictionary is also printed by the Oxford University Press.

*A Dictionary of the English Language*, written single-handedly by Samuel Johnson, was formerly viewed as the pre-eminent English dictionary for use in the United Kingdom. Many years after its introduction, it is still a very helpful dictionary; when it was at its most popular, almost every household had this book on its shelves, and a request for the dictionary would be answered with Johnson's and none other. In fact, at the time, one would ask for the Dictionary just as one asks for the Bible. It is still one of the best English dictionaries, rivalling the Oxford. It is a large dictionary, although not nearly as large as the big Oxford, and, unlike most (*Chambers* being the exception), it is infused with Johnson's trademark dry wit. Owing to its impres-

## 13.2. SUGGESTED DICTIONARIES 115

sive age, Johnson's Dictionary is in the public domain, meaning that it is printed by multiple publishers. It usually fills one or two volumes.

*The Oxford English Dictionary* is by far the largest English dictionary. It is the principal dictionary of the English language, replacing Johnson's in 1928. It consists of twenty volumes, although there is a *Compact Edition of the Oxford English Dictionary* in which the exact text of *The Oxford English Dictionary* is duplicated in very small print. It is intended to be read through the supplied magnifying glass. Reduced in this manner, the dictionary fills two volumes.

For many students, this dictionary may be too comprehensive to use on a regular basis. Huge dictionaries, like this one, can be confusing to some, as the words they use in their definitions are often too big or too rare and make one chase through twenty new words to get the meaning of the original.

Although many students will not use this as their only dictionary, it is a must for every course room and will be found useful in clearing certain words, verifying data from other dictionaries, etc.

It is a valuable reference dictionary and is sometimes the only dictionary that correctly defines a particular word.

## 13.3 Clearing Words

Misunderstoods are remedied by a process called word clearing; this involves the use of a dictionary to find the meaning of a word, and then to use this word in a sentence of one's own to test comprehension. There are two ways to perform word clearing: simply, and by reading aloud.

Simple word clearing is done as follows. When the student recognises that he misunderstands or poorly understands a word, he looks this word up in a dictionary appropriate to his grade level and subject (there exist political, legal, and mathematical dictionaries in which specialist terminology is defined). When the word is found, he copies down or recites the definition that *applies to the word as used* in his own words, after which he attempts to use the word in valid sentences, until he has a clear concept of that meaning of the word.

## 13.3. CLEARING WORDS

Then, the student clears all the other definitions of the word that he does not understand, with the exception of definitions marked *specialised*, *technical*, *obsolete*, or *archaic*, unless the word is being used that way in the context where it was misunderstood. Finally, the student clears the derivation, idioms, and other information given about the word. If any part of the definition contains a further misunderstood word, this must also be cleared before the student may continue. This method is best used with first-language and advanced students.

Reading aloud word clearing, on the other hand, is best done for children and those for whom the language of instruction is different from their own language; it can also be done for advanced students, as it tends to be more reliable than simple word clearing. It is done similarly to the aforementioned simple word clearing; the difference is that difficulties in understanding the meaning are estimated by the supervisor or twin listening to the student read the text aloud; if he hesitates, regularly skips, or makes gross mistakes in the pronunciation of a particular word, this is assumed to be a misunderstood and word clearing proceeds as above. Of course, other reasons for non-optimal reading should be diagnosed and corrected, if there are any; word clearing should not occur in poor light, for example. One of the objects of reading aloud word clearing is to teach the student how to clear words for himself; if he begins to self-clear, this should be furthered, not prevented.

# Chapter 14
# Forms of Study

Books and course packs are historically the most common media from which one studies; in some schools, and on some checksheets, this has remained so. Some schools, however, have course supervisors that are experts in the field they are teaching; these supervisors will often lecture, live and in person, before the class. Other schools place a large emphasis on multi-media presentations, and in this case, they teach the students with audio tapes and compact discs; video tapes and video discs; slide presentations; and the use of computers.

Study using audio or video tapes or discs necessarily has a different feel to it, based on the medium. The same principles, however, apply as for any other form of study. The student must watch out for lack of mass, skipped gradients, and misunderstoods. When studying a tape or a disc, the student does not have the same overview of a whole page or section as he does with written materials. The student is presented with only one part at a time, and he can not see the context in which the idea is presented; this, unfortunately, makes it easier to miss a word or concept.

It is a very good idea to take notes while studying a tape or disc; this ensures retention of the ideas and practices contained therewith (this is called *duplication*), forces the student to think, and puts a small amount of application into the mix. The student should also use his clay and demo kit as appropriate, and often, so that he keeps the necessary balance of mass and significance.

If transcripts are available, they should be used; first of all, they may clarify words that are hard to hear on the tape or disc, but they also combine well with the auditory and visual material of the tapes or discs. A truly multi-media presentation leads to better learning.

Live lectures are, of course, also a form of study; a live lecture has the particular benefit of being personalised. The lecturer can gear his speech to the specific audience being addressed, and he can make demonstrations, such as with clay or by drawing, so that his point is being understood. Unfortunately, a lecture has its disadvantages as well: the lecturer is addressing far more people than just one, and the student may have no say over his speed of delivery. The student may not be able to stop the lecture if he does not understand something, and the lecturer will keep talking even if the student has passed by a misunderstood word.

Since the student can not stop the lecturer, he must be more inventive to avoid the barriers to study; he can prepare for the lecture by orienting himself in terms of the material that will probably be presented, and the key phrases that may be expected. The student should bring a note pad for each lecture. As much as possible, he should evaluate the presented data in terms of category and importance; he can make notes and diagrams in variously-coloured pens, for instance, depending on what he evaluates. The student should note down words and concepts he does not understand, so he can clear them up later.

When given the choice between studying a live or recorded lecture, the student must make the decision very carefully. The live lecture offers more in terms of personalisation, but the taped lecture offers the benefit of being reviewed and cued as much as the student likes, so that he may immediately clear up barriers to study.

# Chapter 15
# Nomenclature

When one is reading and attempting to understand any specialised or technical information, there is one particularly important stumbling block: the nomenclature. The *nomenclature* of a technology (*i.e.*, a coherent body of specialised knowledge) is the jargon, slang, or terminology used by its practitioners.

Unless one understands the words, he does not understand the sentences; unless one understands the sentences, he does not understand the meaning of the printed page or the spoken word. Non-comprehension all comes down to the basic fact that there is a word the student did not understand, or that there is a step he skipped.

There are, of course, two sides to learning new nomenclature. One has to understand the definition itself, and the words and grammar used within it. In addition to this, however, one must compare what is being described to what can be felt or experienced in the world. Does the thing or phenomenon being described actually exist? Can it be observed, felt, or experienced?

Suppose one does research, and, in the process, discovers a new phenomenon; in the spirit of communication, this person wishes to publish what he has discovered. The first thing he must do is devise a nomenclature for this phenomenon, and, more likely than not, the whole technology surrounding it. If he does not do this and simply calls everything 'the thing' or 'the gadget' (this is known as 'Buffy speak', from the television show), the subject will not be clear or practical, and A.R.C. breaks will result simply due to a failure to communicate.

Therefore, nomenclature is necessary. Specialised words can be very useful and helpful in describing new fields, specialised equipment, and newly-discovered facts. Dictionary words may not cover the concepts with enough clarity; in this case, the words may have to be redefined, or new words invented. A new field of knowledge needs its own nomenclature to be clear to its students and to develop in a logical, rational fashion.

If one starts out studying a new subject, he will very soon run into this phenomenon: he will run into a sentence where there is a new, unknown technical word in the middle. If he ignores it or decides to 'catch up' on it later, he will eventually end up in deep trouble as this word is used more and more. If he leaves these technical words behind as misunderstoods, he will very soon realise that he does not have a clue of what the written text means.

Although clearing words one-by-one as they appear may seem slow, this is only an immediate apparency, and looks can be frightfully deceiving. Because misunderstoods tend to slow down the student to a point where he drops the book and 'blows' (isolates himself from the subject), clearing them as they appear is the only way. The immediate effect of bypassing misunderstoods is that one gets slower and slower in his studies.

The student will find that all professions have their own, distinct nomenclature and jargon. On a social level, nomenclatures do much more than define things: they function as a shibboleth—a password to the group—to distinguish the newbies from the old hands.

As mentioned, nomenclature is an important part of the professional's social beingness. The usual cycle is that when a student first enters a field, he will have absorbed all these new terms and will use them to confuse and impress, rather than to elucidate. He will usually be hard to be around for laymen; after a while, however, he will have had his fill, and he will begin to adopt slang expressions for much of his field and nomenclature. He will become more relaxed. Professionals tend to be the most relaxed of all.

For instance, a student doctor may be absolutely incomprehensible to those patients of his that are not also doctors. He wishes to show that he is a trained physician, and that he is a valid member of his group. The experienced veteran, however, will often be found to have put all this behind him. Because he is no longer concerned about being mistaken for a newcomer and has earned his reputation, he can speak to his patients clearly and concisely, use layman's terms when describing things, and he will call a cold a cold.

## 15.1 Double-Speak

In some fields, language is used to obfuscate and to deceive, rather than to illuminate; for this is used the phenomenon known as *double-speak*. Double-speak is very common in fields such as advertising, politics, law, and—occasionally—medicine. Double-speak is written or spoken information that means something other than what it purports to mean; it is distinct from jargon in that jargon is simply specialised nomenclature of a trade or profession. Jargon applies to things which would not be able to be described otherwise, except through Buffy-speak; in contrast, double-speak attempts to make things look better than they really are, and to hide the truth. The truth can be concealed in difficult words or elaborate sentence constructions; it can be embellished by empty adjectives or false comparisons.

There are four main categories of doublespeak: euphemism, jargon, gobbledygook, and inflated language. A euphemism is an inoffensive or positive word or phrase used to avoid an unpleasant reality; examples include *differently-abled* for *disabled*, or *discussing Uganda* for *sexual intercourse* (which is itself a euphemism). Jargon is the specialised nomenclature of a trade or profession, which can also be used to confuse; examples include *malignant carcinoma* for *cancer*, or *rhinovirus* for *common cold*. Gobbledygook, or bureaucratese, is deceptive language used by bureaucrats to overwhelm the audience with long words; examples include *terminological inexactitude* for *untruth*, *police action* for *armed combat*, *enhanced interrogation* for *torture*, *servicing the target* for *bombing*, and *redundancies in human resources* for *layoffs are impending*. Inflated language, which is designed to make an ordinary thing sound impressive, is used mostly by large corporations in job titles; examples include

## 15.1. DOUBLE-SPEAK

*administrative assistant* for *secretary*, *building superintendent* for *janitor*, and *access controller* for *doorman*.

It is important to note that euphemism and jargon do not necessarily indicate double-speak. In a sufficiently advanced field, a technical nomenclature will necessarily become current; similarly, euphemism will always be used, at least to some degree, where people may be offended or taken aback at the harsh reality. Appropriately using jargon and euphemism without the intent to deceive is not double-speak. For example, saying that someone has met his Maker is a perfectly appropriate way to suggest that he has died; this is also true of the phrase "negative patient-care outcome", used all too often in hospitals and medical care facilities. Even the term *sexual intercourse* is a euphemism; the original term for it is originally from the Anglo-Saxon, or Old English, language, and it is now a four-letter word considered *very* vulgar.

The easiest test for double-speak is to write down what the statement at hand implies (what sort of an impression it is trying to leave) and what it truly means. If the two are different, the statement in question is certainly an example of double-speak. However, some examples of double-speak (especially the inflated language used by large businesses) still pass this test, and there is a second test to use. One should ask himself: is there a simpler, more common phrase that is used to mean the same thing? If there is, the phrase in question is again double-speak.

The student must be careful of double-speak, especially in fields such as politics; if he is not, he may find himself strung along into a Kafka-esque world of unending, opaque bureaucracy, like so many others. The student must be able to critically evaluate statements presented to him, read what they say, and understand what they *mean*. The bureaucratese examples above were all drawn from the field of politics (specifically, military politics) with the exception of the last one, which was taken from the world of work; this should give the student an idea of just how common double-speak is in the political arena, and why he should tread carefully.

# Chapter 16
# Balance in Study

Many systems of education have lost sight of the fact that they are there, first and foremost, to prepare the student to apply what he has learned. A student who has been through one of these systems most likely knows all about passing marks and how to earn the professor's respect and goodwill. He knew all about studying long and hard, keeping himself going despite exhaustion. He was taught the content of one textbook after the other, about the ancient history of the subject, and how things were done years ago. He was taught to do long, exhausting calculations. In fact, much of what he was taught seems, to the inexperienced outsider, to be more an intellectual exercise than a practical necessity.

A young man coming out of college usually has some very strange ideas about his eventual hat. His data are theoretical, and he has his relative importances in the wrong order. In most professions, there is a whole culture devoted to 'hazing the newbie', or tricking a rookie into doing the most stupid, but in hindsight hilarious, things. In the Army, for instance, novices are sent to find chemlight batteries (a chemlight is self-sustaining and does not need batteries) or a gun report (the noise made by a firing gun, which is, of course, intangible). In the Navy, the usual fictitious object is batteries for the sound-powered phone (the growler is self-powered and, again, needs no batteries). New nurses are often sent for a neck tourniquet (which would choke and eventually kill the patient), new chemists for dehydrated water (which is nonsense), new musicians for the tacet (Italian for *silence*, not the name of a musical instrumen), new lawyers for verbal agreement forms (which are, by definition, unwritten), and new mechanics for Diesel engine spark plugs (nonsense, as Diesel engines use jets, not spark plugs) or radiator hose for the Volkswagen Beetle (which is air-cooled).

What these conflicting systems of education fail to grasp is that there are three key terms in the field which must be understood and employed, and that these three terms are ever-present in all formal and practical subjects. Any activity or profession has a body of *significances*: the theory and history of the subject, as well as all the explanations and information contained in the textbooks. *Masses* are the physical objects of the field: anything one has to lay his hands on, touch, or move around—the tools, the materials, and the merchandise involved. For example, if one was studying to be an auto mechanic, the mass would be automobiles, engines, and auto parts. *Doingness* is performing and producing in the field: doing all the things that must be done in order to bring about the desired result.

There must be a balance between these three factors to perform well in a field. Good education is about finding this balance and working back and

## 134 CHAPTER 16. BALANCE IN STUDY

forth between theory and practical. The student will eventually acquire the skills necessary to perform and produce in the field. For this, however, there has to be enough significance and theory in place to make the actions understood and to connect with other actions and ojects involved. It is a repeated process that has to take place. There is also a be-do-have sequence that has to take place for this balance to be established firmly and permanently. Once this is established, the student can begin to think with the subject, do new things with it, and adapt what he knows to different situations.

Professionals in any field tirelessly experiment and study basic and new texts in the field. New inventions do not happen overnight, out of the blue, although they are sometimes presented as such. Usually, it will instead be found that someone who suddenly becomes the new sensation has worked at it for years. He has studied, practiced, and studied some more; he has made mistakes; he has progressed slowly, through trial and error and through hard study. Perhaps Thomas Alva Edison, one of the brightest sparks in American history, said it best: "Invention is one per cent. inspiration, and ninety-nine per cent. perspiration."

To become a professional, however, the student does *not* have to go through all the technology that has ever existed in his field, unless he finds it personally interesting. Much of the older technologies should firmly be left in the realm of significance and simply be known. Knowing about them makes the student's thought process more flexible on the subject, to understand the basic principles, and to think *with* the subject.

If a student was required to master all earlier methods before he could move on to the current technology, however, the doingness would become a significance, leaving the student wondering what the point of it is. Hunting deer with bow and arrow may be fun, and a technology all its own, but unless the student wishes to learn this old way in practice, it is sufficient to learn *about* it.

# Chapter 17
# Levels of Engagement

Part of understanding a textbook for professional purposes is to understand the nomenclature; there is no substitute for this, and in subjects with extensive nomenclature, this, unfortunately, must simply be sweated out. The reward for doing so is an intimate knowledge of the phenomena described therein.

There are, however, a number of ways a subject can be approached; the student can, for instance, get into a subject with no intention of becoming an expert in, or practitioner of, it. Before embarking

## CHAPTER 17. LEVELS OF ENGAGEMENT

on a field of study, the student must make it clear, to himself, what his purpose is in learning it. Having done so, he can choose the books, classes, and methods that suit him.

First of all, though, the student must simply *be there* mentally, as well as physically. To ensure that students are in the classroom mentally, the supervisor may do what L.R.H. termed the Locational Process. The supervisor stands in front of the class, and asks the students, as a group, to point to (say) a particular wall. After they have done so, he acknowledges and thanks them, and asks them to point to (say) a particular desk. The supervisor may have the students touch objects, shake each others' hands, stomp on the floor. The goal of all this is to make absolutely, undeniably clear to the student that he is in the classroom, mentally and physically. It helps make the student more focussed, and more capable of listening to the supervisor/teacher. Again, the very lowest level of engagement is being there, and this is actually very important.

Another way to apply this datum is by making an *orientation checksheet*; this can be done on a student's first day, and simply consists of giving him a list of places to find, such as classrooms and offices. This process helps the student realise, mentally, that he is at a new place, and the lay-out of this new place. It also comes in handy when one has poor orientation and always gets lost; doing a checksheet of this sort, until the layout of the place is mastered, will definitely improve one's orientation and will cut down on time spent asking for directions.

The next level of knowledge is *knowing a few scraps*. One may simply wish to know about a subject enough to recognise it when it is mentioned on the news or in casual conversation. This level of knowledge can be obtained from reading an encyclopædia, or even a good dictionary.

After this comes the *ability to talk about it socially*, building on the above. To attain this, one can read popular magazine articles on the subject to learn the newest and latest in the field. One may also learn some of its nomenclature so he can demonstrate his knowledge and have intercourse with its experts.

Then comes *dilettantism*; a dilettante is essentially a dabbler, which can be an unfortunate state of affairs if there is an element of pretended knowledge and skill involved, or if the student is trying to fool others or himself. However, here is where doingness becomes a factor.

The *practical worker* has learned skills in the field, usually by following the examples set by another. This does not involve deep understanding of the subject, but the student can be of great use and create good products in his area of competence (not to be confused with expertise).

The *informed customer*, in addition to the above, has learned skills in fields bordering on his area of competence; he wishes to know enough about a field to be able to talk and have business intercourse with professionals. A sailor, for instance, may wish to know about meteorology so that he may predict the weather; he may also wish to know about cartography, so he may understand the charts he uses.

One can have extensive *theoretical knowledge* on a subject, including its full nomenclature. This type of knowledge is required especially by its so-called experts and professors; they may not, however, be capable of practice in the field, as they do not have the practical skills required. This is a valid level of knowledge, although it has its shortcomings; experts are called upon by professional buyers and practitioners, so that they may receive the one piece of infomation they need. Theoretical knowledge is laden with significances, but light on doingness and application; it does have an important purpose of its own, as it preserves knowledge that otherwise may get lost, due to its apparent practical irrelevance.

The *practitioner* balances significance, doingness, mass, theory, and practice well. He studies a level of skill, practices that level for a while, studies the next level, practices that, and so on.

A practitioner who keeps studying and applies what he learns will eventually become a true *professional*. He will know most of what there is to know about a field, and he will be able to perform all the skills described in the theory in a competent manner, adding 'that little extra touch'.

Study Technology is useful to all these competence levels, but sees as its ultimate purpose to bring about true professionalism. Professionals are needed in any field of lasting value. This is the level of competence upon which life and death are balanced. Hospitals without professionals in the operating theatre will lose patients, for instance. The society at large needs professionals to survive.

# Chapter 18

# Out-points and Plus-points

Critical thinking is a very important skill to master. The student must be able to understand that not everything which is written down as a book is in any way workable or true; he must be able to evaluate material on its merits, and not because someone told him that the material is true. In furtherance of this end, L.R.H. developed three concepts that help the student think critically: the *ideal scene*, *out-points*, and *plus-points*.

The ideal scene, in its basic concept, is a clean statement of its purpose; for instance, it may be the state of affairs envisioned to be the best obtainable reality. The ideal scene for this course, as described on its checksheet, is *an able student who knows how to study, has the knowledge and tools to be able to study and apply the materials of any course, and uses this knowledge.*

An out-point is something that is wrong with an ideal scene; usually, it comes in the form of a datum that does not add up right. An out-point does not mean that the data are false, but the outnesses must be considered as such. They subtract from the ideal scene, as they misalign with the stated purpose or goal.

Plus-points are the converse of out-points: they indicate something right, and act as elements of the ideal scene. A plus-point shows that data are in good order; it shows something that is right. They help obtain the ideal scene, as they align with the stated purpose or goal.

There are eleven out-points, and they are listed below:

1. *An omitted datum or thing:* A datum, fact, or anything that *should* be there, but is missing.

2. *Altered sequence*: Things are explained, happening, or done out of their logical sequence. Doing a series of steps in the order 4, 2, 1, 5, 3 is this.

3. *Dropped time*: *When* something happened or should be done is not mentioned. Not following, or not posting, opening hours is this.

4. *Falsehood*: A false datum, a deception, a pretense, a lie.

5. *Altered importance*: Facts are given the wrong value and importance. Comments are made into all-important statements of fact.

6. *Wrong target*: Fixing the wrong thing is a wrong target. So is blaming or attacking the wrong people. Even completely misunderstanding with whom you are trying to communicate can be this. It is often due to mistaken identity.

7. *Wrong source*: After a fashion, this is the converse of a wrong target. Information, orders, or gifts taken from the wrong source can add up to eventual confusion and possible trouble.

8. *Contrary facts*: Two or more data that can not both be true; at least one is false. This is a type of false data, but which one is false is yet to be determined.

9. *Added time*: This means using much more time than estimated or reasonable.

10. *Added inapplicable data*: Data that is in no way applicable to the scene or situation—it does not apply to the subject at hand.

11. *Incorrectly included datum*: A datum from one class of data is included wrongly in another class.

Plus-points are the opposite of out-points. They are used and classified the same way as the outpoints, but here, we are isolating the positive aspects of the situation, technology, or activity. The fourteen plus-points are:

1. Related facts known (all relevant facts in hand);
2. Events in correct sequence;
3. Time noted;
4. Data proven factual;
5. Correct relative importance;
6. Expected time period;
7. Adequate data;
8. Applicable data;
9. Correct source;
10. Correct target;
11. Data in same classification;
12. Identities are identical, not similar or different;

13. Similarities are similar, not identical or different; and

14. Differences are different, not similar or identical.

# Chapter 19

# What is a Course?

In schools, students are taught technologies (areas of study, such as chemistry, English literature, sociology, and study itself) in courses. There are certain things a course should have, and there are things it should not have; in fact, these things may be so important that they are crucial for the course to actually be a course. When teaching a course using the Study Technology, the teacher-supervisor's responsibility is to ensure that the course is doing its job.

First of all, a course needs a checksheet. The

reason a course needs a checksheet is so that there is no confusion regarding what needs to be studied and in what order. Classes taught in the traditional way also use a checksheet, after a fashion; however, in traditional courses, the checksheet is held by the supervisor, items on it are released one at a time, and the checksheet is shared by all the students of a course. The effect of this is that the students with greater natural aptitude for the course are stuck waiting for their slower peers, and the slower students are hurried in their study. If every student is given an individual checksheet, this does not happen.

A course also needs materials. Materials, in addition to lectures, is what students learn from. Materials can take many forms; they can be bound into a book, they can be printed on loose leaf paper, they can be a computer file, or they can be lectures on a compact disc. Taken as a group, the materials needed for a student's study are termed the *course pack*; each student must have one full course pack. In addition to the course pack, materials include the resources shared among the class: clay, tables and chairs, computers, pink sheets, the attendance book, demo kits, dictionaries standard, technical, and polyglot, etc. All of this must be in place for the course to deserve its name.

Furthermore, a course needs a supervisor. The supervisor, in addition to being trained in his field of expertise, should be trained in the methods and practices of Study Technology. The duties of the supervisor are to ensure that students are present, and that the methods of Study Technology are being properly applied. He fills out pink sheets for students, ensures that the students comprehend every word of their materials as well as the concepts these words form, and he remedies insufficient mass by bringing it into the classroom, as a model or otherwise, or by bringing the students to the mass. Discipline is also necessary; what a shame it would be to have an excellent course, but with the students throwing paper aeroplanes at the supervisor and making so much noise that those who are actually interested in the subject can not hear themselves think. The supervisor is responsible for maintaining discipline.

Discipline often comes in the form of rules and guidelines, although an adage states that rules were meant to be broken. This is, in a way, true; dogmatically interpreted rules have been the death of many a good organisation. For this reason, the supervisor is charged not only with enforcing the rules of good study practice, but also with ensuring that they are applied with sound judgement.

Each course has its own separate rules; a nursing programme, for instance, may have a rule on what to do when unlabelled, loose medication is found on the floor. A police fundamentals programme will not need such a rule, but they most certainly will have rules on the interrogation of detainees.

There are, however, rules which apply to a broad variety of subjects; as such, they can be enforced irrespective of which course is being taught. Besides the unwritten rules of common courtesy, such as not speaking out of turn, there are rules whose purpose is simply to promote good study skills.

1. Students represent the school at which they study; therefore, they ought to behave accordingly.

2. One should be a student when he studies, a teacher when he teaches or supervises, and a professional when he applies his field.

3. Students are to breakfast before morning class every day; they are to start the course clean, well-rested, and well-fed.

4. Students are to get adequate sleep. Contrary to popular belief, there is no substitute, whether pharmaceutical or behavioural, for sleep.

5. Students must not drink any alcohol, nor take any barbiturates, cannabinoids, benzodiazepines, or zopiclone analogue drugs for twenty-four hours before each lesson. Medications such as these are known as depressants of the central nervous system; they dull the faculties, making it difficult to absorb and retain information.

6. Students are to moderate their use of psychoanaleptics (such as caffeine, amphetamine, and piracetam) and opiates (mor-

phine) while on course. If used frequently or at a high dose, these drugs can cause sleep disturbances.

7. In case of misunderstandings, confusion, or ignorance about some part of the course, students are to clear this up with their supervisor.

8. Students must give advanced notice for a leave of absence from course. Students must sign out before leaving and sign in after returning.

9. Students are to refrain from causing undue noise in the building.

10. Students are to use correct entrances to, and egresses from, the building.

11. Students are to treat courseroom furniture and material with respect.

12. Students shall not eat, store food, or smoke in course rooms.

The final, and most necessary, part of a course is its students. If a course is scheduled properly, teaches a valid, workable technology, and is run well, it will attract many students. The students will know that they will learn the materials, and that they will progress. If the course is not run properly, it will either end up deserted, with the supervisor watching an empty classroom, or it will end up full, but with students that are there simply to kill time and that, by the course's end, have learned nothing.

If the course has just a few students sitting on broken chairs, throwing wadded-up paper around, and an ineffectual supervisor that allows and encourages this to happen, it might as well not be called a course. A course should produce graduates that know what they are doing.

# Chapter 20
# Running a Course

There are two ways a course can be run. It can be run efficiently, with ethics being present (or 'in'), or it can be run inefficiently, with ethics being absent (or 'out').

An efficiently-run course has a schedule that is strictly adhered to. Each major study period is started with roll call. There is a course schedule and it is strictly adhered to. The supervisor is diligent in applying Study Technology. He sets daily targets for each of the students; he discusses the checksheet items briefly with the student, noting any familiarity with the materials, and with this in mind sets a realistic target for the student to reach. The points system should not be used on its own to set targets with; it is merely a statistic to see trends in the student's work. The ultimate target, of course, is to graduate the student.

In the efficiently-run course, the supervisor observes his students as they study. From time to time, he writes his observations on a pink sheet, and if there are poor study habits present, he fills in the assignment column. The pink sheet is handed to the student regardless of whether there is an assignment.

The easiest way to tell if the course is not being run efficiently is to peek in the classroom. If there are students wandering around and socialising instead of studying properly, if students arrive late for roll-call and are not disciplined for this, if students take cigarette breaks often and without permission, the course is definitely not being run with the least bit of efficiency and discipline. In an undisciplined course, it will be found that some sort of group agreement has developed that makes the lack of discipline seem normal and the way things are supposed to be. When a new student walks in, he will see all this and, more often than not, fall into line with this lack of discipline.

Students that attend this sort of course will become poor practitioners; they will not keep appointments or apply technology correctly, and they will themselves fail to keep discipline.

Any supervisor allowing the following to take place does not deserve his title, and needs to be reprimanded or dismissed.

- Omitting roll call of his students in the morning and after lunch, as well as between classes, on time. He does not take note of students being absent, and does not take corrective action when they are.

- Permitting students to socialise, wander around, take unscheduled breaks, or sit idle during class

- Permitting students to eat, or, worse, smoke in the courseroom

- Permitting people to come into the courseroom and interrupt students

- Supervisor standing around or sitting at his desk, doing essentially nothing

- Supervisor does not assist students' progress through the course and does not promote their graduation.

# Chapter 21
# The Points System

Whether supervising, teaching, or learning, it is often helpful to chart the student's progress; to do this, the points system is used. A points system is an arbitrary system, created either by the author of the material or by the course supervisor, that assigns an arbitrary number of effort points to the student for completing certain tasks.

For instance, each page of text read may be worth one point. A check-out on a study unit (a chapter, section, or other such unit of text) may be worth ten points; passing this check-out may be worth an additional five points. For this particular course, the points system may be found in the front of the pack, after the pink sheet masters and before the checksheets.

Each time the student does an action listed on the points chart, the appropriate number of points is added to his running daily count for the course, as well as a separate total daily count. When the course is over for the day, as well as when the day is over, the final count is plotted on a graph.

Graphs are usually constructed with the independent variable on the $x$ axis and the dependent variable on the $y$ axis. The independent variable affects, but is not affected by, the dependent variable. When graphing effort points, the independent variable is time. It does not matter if students study more or less; tomorrow will come either way. The date, therefore, goes on the $x$ axis. Effort points are the dependent variable. Changing the date may change the number of effort points awarded, since students have good days and bad days. The number of daily points, therefore, goes on the $y$ axis.

The trend in points obtained over time is also

known as the *stat*, from the word *statistics*. If the number of effort points obtained is rising, the student is *up-stat*. If the trend is falling, the student is *down-stat*. The course supervisor, as well as students themselves, ought to look at the points graphs regularly (at least fortnightly).

If the student finds himself down-stat, he should meet with his supervisor, his parents, his friends, and anyone else involved with his education, and they should assist the student in finding the deeper reason for his down-statness. Similarly, if the student finds that he is consistently up-stat, day after day, he may also wish to meet with his supervisor and others involved with his education, so that he may find the cause of his up-statness.

# Chapter 22

# Pink Sheets: A Supervisor's Perspective

In the course of his duties, the properly-trained supervisor will need to fill out what is known as a pink sheet. An invaluable teaching tool, pink sheets allow the student to judge his study as well as his teaching from a detached, third-person perspective. The student should look forward to receiving pink sheets, and he should receive them often;

## CHAPTER 22. PINK SHEETS (SUPERVISORS)

consequently, they are *never* to be used as punishment.

A standard pink sheet, as devised by R. Hubbard, is composed of four columns: one each for the names of the supervisor, student, and his teacher, and one for the supervisor's observations. Pink sheets are best printed on pink paper; doing otherwise is likely to lead to confusion. The observations column is the most important of the four, as this is what the pink sheet system, as a method of instruction, rests upon. The use of a pink sheet is described below; it takes, however, far more than instruction from written material—namely, practice and experience—to write one that best benefits the student. Pink sheets should be ubiquitous in the classroom, and need not direct the student to take corrective action, although this certainly is a possibility.

To use a pink sheet, the supervisor walks up to a pair of students teaching each other, standing close enough to see and hear, and far enough so as not to be intrusive or obnoxious. He takes two copies of the pink sheet, one of which should be a colour other than pink, and slides a sheet of carbon paper between them. At this point, he is ready to begin. He writes the names of the student, supervisor, teacher, and school in the spaces at the top of the sheet, and is now ready to begin. The supervisor now observes, and notes his observations in the appropriate column as they happen. At this time, it is not the role of the supervisor to call attention to any mistakes; he is there simply to *be there*, show interest in the teaching session, and impartially observe and record the study habits, body language, and/or speech patterns of the students. He records what is being studied and how it is being studied. If there are signs of non-comprehension, of course, the supervisor must note them down, but not to the exclusion of everything else.

When the supervisor has finished his observations, he evaluates the students; he makes sure that they have not missed anything. Potential pitfalls may include a drill that is difficult for a particular student, weak materials revealed by a check-out, a concept that the student is unable to demonstrate (this is a sign of non-comprehension, as intangible things can certainly be represented with a study kit or clay), or even hesitation or pronunciation difficulties with one particular word. If anything needs correction, the course supervisor fills in the assignment portion of the pink sheet, noting down exactly what must be studied.

For instance, if the student can not demonstrate a particular person, thing, situation, or idea, his task would be to figure out a way to do so, perhaps back-tracking through his materials as he does. If he has misunderstood a word, the pink sheet should be written to make him clear it. If he shows a lack of comprehension of a particular gradient and has obviously skipped an earlier one, the proper sequence of gradients should be pointed out on the pink sheet.

Regardless of whether or not anything has been assigned, the pink half of the pink sheet (the original) is given to the student. The carbon copy, which may be printed on blue or yellow paper, goes into the supervisor's course folder. When the student has finished with the original (in the absence of an assignment, having read over it carefully), it is filed in the student's personal folder.

If a student has received a pink sheet assignment, it should be done with a twin, whether it is theory, practical, or both. The twin first reviews the observations with the student; then, he star-rates the student on the issues as assigned and drills the student until the correct data are completely learned and understood. Once this is done, the twin initials the column labelled COACH; the student is now ready to hand the pink sheet in to the supervisor.

The student now turns his pink sheet in to the supervisor. This must be done in person, as the supervisor may wish to go over it with the student and check him out himself. In doing this, the supervisor wishes to know if the pink sheet has done its job, or if he has to keep a closer eye on the student or do remedial work with him.

Pink sheets must never be used as punishment or to convince the student that he is wrong. They are used to improve the student's study or teaching ability by having him re-study data and do practical drills in the weak areas. A student's weakness in data and skills will often not show up under the normal conditions of theory study and practical drilling, but they will stand out very sharply when the time comes to apply what he has learned.

# Chapter 22. Pink Sheets (Supervisors)

Therefore, a pink sheet assignment does not necessarily mean that the student did not study the material properly, even if he has already passed it in theory or practical. It does mean that he has not learned it well enough to use it under the duress of an actual situation. If a student has gone a few days without receiving a pink sheet, he should start asking for one. Pink sheets ensure that study results in a string of certainties—the basic tenet of Study Technology. It may take several times over the material to be able to do things correctly, and under trying conditions, in practice.

# Chapter 23

# Writing Course Materials

One of the best and most valuable assets a course may have is a supervisor who is an expert and true professional in the course he is teaching. If this is true of a supervisor, he may not only supervise the course, but also teach in the traditional sense. Of course, he must not forsake one of his duties for the other; the course must still, in order to be efficient, be run in accordance with the basic tenets of Hubbard's Study Technology.

If the supervisor is qualified to do so, one of the best ways to teach a course is by writing the materials it uses, rather than having to give the same talks to the students, year after year. The course pack, however, must be written in a particular way to appeal to students, to broaden their understanding, and to quicken their minds.

The first step, which is rather obvious, is to avoid out-points. Having out-points in a coursepack renders it questionable; the basic thinking of the student in this regard is that if the author missed the out-points, he might have also missed some crucial part of the subject, or simply does not know what he is talking about.

Using technical nomenclature to obfuscate, rather than illuminate, can also present a problem to the readership. What is here being referred to is not double-speak, but merely literary pretention: the author either feels that complex or Latinate words are inherently better than simple or Saxon ones, or else he (mistakenly) assumes that employing such long words makes him a better or more sophisticated writer. George Orwell, author of *1984* and *Animal Farm* made his thoughts very clear on the subject:

> Except for [certain] useful abbreviations, there is no real need for any of the hundreds of foreign phrases now current in the English language. Bad writers, and especially scientific, political, and sociological writers, are nearly always haunted by the notion that Latin or Greek words are grander than Saxon ones, and unnecessary words like *expedite, ameliorate, predict, extraneous, deracinated, clandestine, subaqueous*, and hundreds of others constantly gain ground. [...] An interesting illustration of this is the way in which English flower names were in use till very recently are being ousted by Greek ones, *snapdragon* becoming *antirrhinum, forget-me-not* becoming myosotis, etc. It is hard to see any practical reason for this change of fashion: it is probably due to an instinctive turning away from the more homely word

and a vague feeling that the Greek word is scientific.

Of course, double-speak itself must be avoided, especially in a teaching setting; the exception would be in a jurisprudence or political science course, where the student must be able to detect, understand, and strategically employ double-speak in situations which call for it. The prohibition against double-speak is over-ridden by the positive mandate to teach and learn for application; ¡@@@¿

The major problem to avoid, however, is a *dogmatic* tone of writing. The *Oxford English Dictionary* defines the term *dogma* as *a principle or set of principles laid down by an authority as incontrovertibly true*. If a statement is presented as true without any background or reference offered, it is likely to be dogma, unless the book is written at a high enough gradient to obviate the need for such background, or a low enough gradient to be below the gradient of the background.

For example, an algebra textbook does not need to explain or prove the fact that one plus one equals two. An astronomy textbook for university use does not need to explain or prove the roundness of the Earth. Basic textbooks in these two areas would need to explain this and much more. Conversely, but similarly, 'primer' books come below the gradient of the texts they serve as introductions to: one is expected to read the primer before he reads the official text. If the student, in addition to reading the primer, is made aware of the need to read the official text, references to the official text are not necessary.

Good academic writing should also be written with a focus towards application, not theory; although a little biographical information is needed about Isaac Newton in a physics course, it should not become the focus of a physics course, and the student must not be tested on it. The Ideal Scene of a course is to have its student proficient in the practice of a particular technology; the designer of the course must keep in mind that the Ideal Scene of a physics course is to make the student a physicist, not a biographer.

Appropriate mass must be included in the course materials; pictures, models, and audio or video discs are crucial for the understanding of the student. The Ideal Scene for mass in the course is the inclusion of the actual thing being studied. Just below the Ideal Scene is the inclusion of computers in the course; in fact, computers are sometimes more valuable than the study mass, as they can be set to replicate any version thereof, and in the case of certain mission-critical fields of study, computers allow the technology to be studied without threat of injury to human life.

As an example, imagine a student wishes to fly heavy passenger and cargo jets. He has already received his basic pilot credentials (meaning he can fly piston aircraft with a single engine), his instrument flight rating (meaning he can fly blind), his multiple-engine credentials, and his commercial pilot licence (meaning he can carry more than a certain number of passengers or weight of goods, or any passengers or goods for compensation). He has two routes: he can learn to fly in real Airbus, Boeing, Fokker, and Embraer machines, or he can learn to fly a computer-based simulator with the cockpits and handling styles of each of these aircraft. The computer, while possibly not perfect, will allow him to crash the plane as much as is required without injuring a single soul.

The checksheet must be written in the order that the course should be learned; basic topics must precede more advanced ones. The course pack, however, also should be in the same order: the student should not be made to flip back and forth between pages trying to find the chapter or research paper he is looking for. This is especially important if the course pack is in book form, rather than being loose-leaf pages in a binder or folder, since a book can not be reärranged.

Prospective authors should note that the best authority on a technology (a system of beliefs and practices used to accomplish something) is often its originator, as all later innovations came from the groundwork that he lay. The benefit of using primary sources can not be stressed enough. For instance, no psychoänalysis text would be complete without something by Sigmund Freud. The pack for a physics course should include the works of Isaac Newton, translated into English.

Of course, out-dated ideas should not be taught, unless they are taught with a footnote stating that they are of historical interest only. For instance, the works of Faraday and Ohm were partially superseded by the work of Maxwell, who unified their discoveries into a single theory of electromagnetism. Similarly, the study of optics and classical mechanics would best be served by the works of Isaac Newton. Where Newton's work is incorrect, Planck, Einstein, and Bohr can take over.

Therefore, there is no shame in simply compiling the best parts of several different experts, or in expanding upon the work of one such expert. Of course, this is only practical in advanced courses, where the students are familiar with the necessary background materials; high-school students would be hard-pressed to understand the works of Newton or Einstein. A compilation such as this should, of course, include the necessary tools to help the student; ideally, a skeleton text would be built around the primary sources, anchoring the disparate papers to a stable base.

Therefore, there is no shame in simply compiling the best parts of several different experts, or in expanding upon the work of one such expert. Of course, this is only practical in advanced courses, where the students are familiar with the necessary background materials; high-school students would be hard-pressed to understand the works of Newton or Einstein. A compilation such as this should, of course, include the necessary tools to help the student; ideally, a skeleton text would be built around the primary sources, anchoring the disparate papers to a stable base.

Regardless of whether or not this approach is followed, the course author needs to pay special attention to the checklist and the points system. Although the instructional part of the course pack teaches the student what something is, and how and why it works, the checklist serves as proof of his abilities in this area. No textbook is complete without questions to test whether the student truly understands what he is studying; in Hubbardian Study Technology, these questions are put on a checksheet, rather than dispersed throughout the text. A more fundamental difference between the questions on a checksheet and the questions in some of today's textbooks are that checksheet questions screen for application. The checksheet has a secondary purpose: it allows students, teachers, and parents to gauge the student's progress into the course. If one is in the middle of a checksheet, he should also be in the middle of a course.

The points system, on the other hand, is designed to gauge the student's progress per unit time, a discipline known as statistics, or stats. The student's statistics change based on internal and external factors; the goal for all concerned is to keep the statistics rising. As with the rest of Hubbard's Study Technology, the points system should be skewed towards application, to a greater or lesser degree. There is a points system for both the Study and Supervisor Hat Courses; for technologies which learn through other media than that listed, or in other such scenarios, a new points system can be devised.

# Glossary

**Checksheet** A list of materials, often divided into sections, that give the theory and practical steps which, when completed, give one a study completion. The items are selected to add up to the required knowledge of the subject. They are arranged in the sequence necessary to a gradient of increasing knowledge of the subject. After each item, there is a place for the initial of the student or the person checking the student out. When the checksheet is fully initialled, it is complete, meaning the student may now take an exam and be granted the award for completion.

**Checklist** A list of actions or inspections to ready

an activity or machinery or object for use or estimate the needful repairs or corrections. This is erroneously sometimes called a *checksheet*, but that word is reserved for study steps.

**Check-out** The action of verifying a student's knowledge of an item given on a checksheet.

**Check-out, twin** When two students are paired they check each other out. This is different than a Supervisor checkout.

**Check-out, supervisor** A checkout done by the Supervisor of a course or his assistants.

**Theory** The data part of a course, where the data, as in books, tapes and manuals, are given.

**Practical** The drills which permit the student to associate and coordinate theory with the actual items and objects to which the theory applies. Practical is application of what one knows to what one is being taught to understand, handle or control.

**Out** Things which should be there and are not, or should be done and are not, are said to be out.

**In** Things which should be there and are or should be done and are, are said to be in.

**Pack** A pack is a collection of written materials which match a checksheet. It is variously constituted—it can be loose leaf, a cardboard folder, or pages in a Duo-Tang. A pack does not necessarily include a booklet or hardcover book that may be called for as part of a checksheet.

**Manual** A booklet of instruction for a certain object, procedure or practice.

**Points** The arbitrary assignment of a credit value to a part of study materials. A page of study materials, a chapter from a book, or an item on a checksheet can all be worth an arbitrary number of points.

**Point system** The system of assigning and counting up points for studies and drills that give the progress of a student and measure his speed of study. They are kept track of by the student and Course Administrator and added up each week as the student's statistic. The statistic of the course is the combined study points of the class, divided by the number of students.

**Completion** A *completion* occurs when a course has been started, worked through, and has successfully ended with a summative assignment or examination (*Qual*) and consequent award.

**Cause, to be at** To be in control of; to be able to change. From cause-effect relationships; you are the cause of change in something. For instance, one can be at cause over his finances, his education, his life.

**Effect, to be at** To be at the mercy of; to be powerless to change. From cause-effect relationships; something has an effect on you, which you can not be the cause of. One can be at effect over his studies if he does not understand how to educate himself properly.

**Mass** An object being studied, in its physical form and "beingness", has mass; the object itself can also be called a mass. Representations of this object, such as pictures, also have mass, although they have less mass than the object itself. Some mass is needed to learn.

**Gradient** The progression of ideas in a course of study, from easiest to most difficult. Also, each individual idea in this progression. Gradients must be mastered in the order they appear.

**Misunderstood** A word, idea, or concept which is not understood, or which is poorly understood. Misunderstoods can cause noncomprehension of a critical point upon which the study depends, and if this happens, the study will be compromised. Misunderstoods are remedied by looking them up in a dictionary.

**Inflow** Information going 'into' a subject's

mind; listening and reading are methods of inflow.

**Outflow** Information going 'out of' a subject's mind; originating communication in some way. Talking, writing, and gesturing are methods of outflow; and so is performing actions, as well as teaching them to others.

**Stuck flow** A situation that results when an incorrectly taught student (too much emphasis on inflow) must demonstrate his knowledge and is unable to.

**Hat** One's role or job; an individual wears multiple hats throughout the course of the day, switching between them. The activity one is engaged in at a given moment usually has a hat associated with it, and this hat has rules and practices associated with it. Jobs are paid; hats may or may not be.

www.ingramcontent.com/pod-product-compliance
Lightning Source LLC
Chambersburg PA
CBHW071415160426
43195CB00013B/1696